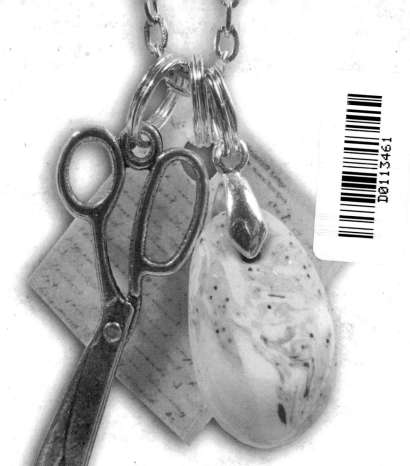

ROCK PAPER SCISSORS

GOD'S MIGHTY POWER,
JESUS' COVERING FORGIVENESS, AND THE
SNIPPING REFINEMENT OF THE HOLY SPIRIT

Alison M. Sullivan

Praise for Rock Paper Scissors

"In writing honestly of herself instead of assuming about others, Sullivan's unique voice is relatable and poignant, sans finger pointing. Sullivan shows, not tells, through snapshots of her own life and observations that broadcasting our shortcomings is fun, winsome, and all the more celebratory of the God who works in spite of them."

—CALLIE ZINSMEYER, *recent college graduate teeter-tottering between "faith that glorifies God through fearless dreams" versus "doing small things with great love;" a big sister, friend, amateur yogi, and wandering sheep.*

"*Rock Paper Scissors* is a fresh revelation of the extravagant love of God, the amazing grace of Jesus, the intimate friendship of the Holy Spirit. Without limiting the awesomeness of God, Sullivan has a way of communicating Biblical truths we all wrestle with that makes living out our faith without excuses seem like something we can actually do! Carefully filtered through the fingers of the Holy Spirit, this book is hilarious yet deep, profound yet simple. Sullivan captures how God reveals himself in our every day lives, and shows us how getting out of our comfort zones allows us to know Him better. Inspiring! Honest! Obedient! *Rock Paper Scissors* resonated with my own struggles and awakened my soul."

—STACIE CAFFEY, *wife to an amazing man, mother to 3 wild and crazy kids; labor and delivery nurse who enjoys designing and decorating but is afraid no one will like her ideas; saved at age 8 but lost as a goose until her early 30s, and on a mission to serve our Lord Jesus well every day.*

"There is such beauty in the surrender of one's life, and there is nothing more beautiful than surrendering your life to let God use it. These brave, beautiful words will bring so much freedom to anyone who reads them. Through a mixture of vulnerability interwoven with stories of a life forever changed by grace, this book invites you to be encouraged at the core of your soul. Sullivan's words bring many laughs, tears, understanding, and leave you with a heart filled with encouragement."

—AMANDA ROSSY, *recent college graduate who struggles with seeing herself through the Lord's eyes instead of the world's eyes; continuously reminded that the Lord's plans are better than anything she could ever dream up on her own.*

"*Rock Paper Scissors,* is written by a self-proclaimed 'non-writer.' It is authentic, honest, and raw. Peppered with relatable, thought-provoking (and often hysterical) anecdotes, the heart behind this book is clear... we are deeply and passionately loved by our Savior, and having an intimate, growing relationship with Him is all He desires of us. I plan on reading everything this 'non-writer' writes!"

—ASHLEY JENKINS, *married to her best friend, raising two fun-loving, silly boys, passionate about learning the details of others' lives; claims to like ironing but really it's the only way she can watch TV during the day without feeling guilty; currently learning that the Lord's ways are higher than her own and trying to trust that all things really do work together for good; and above all, a cherished daughter of the King.*

"Sullivan's 'kitchen table theology' is practical, real, impactful, and not at all preachy! Her vulnerability about her own faith journey and discoveries of God will invite you into her life and her love for the Lord with a wink and a wry smile. You will feel like you're sitting across her kitchen table hearing her stories first hand, letting you know that you're not alone in this journey! This is a must-read, and a must-pass-on as well!"

—KELLEY MULLINS, *rookie Youth Minister, still a sinner; self-proclaimed warrior, God-proclaimed toddler; lover of music, animals and babies; struggles with both cynicism and idealism, hoping for hope.*

"*Rock Paper Scissors* is thought provoking and honest and challenges readers to step outside of their comfort zone in order to draw closer to God. Sullivan is as wise as she is relatable. This book is one you will want to share with your book club and read again and again!"

—ANDREA PUSKAR, *mother of three, wanna be philanthropist, actual stay at home mom, possible Christian, comfortably spiritual, constantly seeking.*

"Sullivan's authenticity, humor, and deeply important insight into the difference between a Jesus-centered life and a Christian culture-centered one is a digestible and wise message the church desperately needs to hear. Bravo!"

—JANET DAVIS, *author of The Feminine Soul, Sacred Healing and My Own Worst Enemy*

About the Author

Allison M. Sullivan resides in Bryan, Texas with her husband, Seth, and their four children, Sylas, Amelia, Blaise, and Wren (plus one on the way from Haiti). While in the trenches of motherhood she is currently applying her teaching degree in Special Education and her masters degree in Cynology outside of the classroom. She enjoys teaching yoga, her ministry with college women, dates with her husband, good books, soulful music, car dancing with her kids, and ferocious friendships with faithful women. *Rock Paper Scissors* is her first book.

ROCK
PAPER
SCISSORS

God's Mighty Power,
Jesus' Covering Forgiveness,
and the Snipping Refinement
of the Holy Spirit

Allison M. Sullivan

2015
GREEN PUBLISHING HOUSE, LLC
College Station, Texas

Rock Paper Scissors.

ISBN 978-1-63432-025-2 (paperback)
ISBN 978-1-63432-026-9 (epub)
ISBN 978-1-63432-027-6 (pdf)
ISBN 978-1-63432-028-3 (mobi)
ISBN 978-1-63432-029-0 (audio)

Biblical references listed in the text are cited from the New American Standard Bible.

www.GreenPublishingHouse.com

Dedication

In loving memory of Terry Bilhartz and Steve Sullivan,
who left this earth empty because
they poured themselves out.

Sue Ann -
you are perfectly
crafted.
Shine bright,
Allison
Sui

Table of Contents

Introduction

"Faith is one foot on the ground, one foot in the air,
and a queasy feeling in the stomach."
—MOTHER ANGELICA

When I try to start something new, the voice I hear first says, "But what if it doesn't work?"

In the writing of this book, that thought has plagued me.

Because, you see, I am not a real writer. Not for an audience anyway. Scratching out a rhyming to-do list over posting a witty tweet, a journal entry over an article submission, fine-tuning an email over editing a chapter, I like to write, but when I do, I pretend that no one is reading.

Real writers have sharp wit, are a bit on the eccentric side, and are, perhaps, a little melancholy. They have pet cats. Real writers know when to use "I" versus "me" and "who" versus "whom." They sit in coffee shops for peaceful hours on peaceful end. They are scholarly and wear trendy glasses. And most importantly, people read what real writers have to say.

Hardly any of these attributes describe me.

I have the occasional witty *moment*, but it is just that: a moment. I celebrate it wildly. I tend to lean toward the cheerful side. I was never all that great at school. I barely use prepositions and I don't know what a gerund is. I prefer dogs to cats. I am raising four kids, five and under, and have nary a peaceful hour, certainly not on end, so any visit to a coffee shop is out of pure necessity. I have 20/20 vision and no need for trendy glasses. I once kept a blog that only a couple handfuls of faithful friends ever read. I do not feel like a real writer.

And yet, God didn't seem to care. Because the idea of this book? Well, it just wouldn't go away... which is pretty inconvenient when you don't think of yourself as one who writes.

In order to finish this book, I had to keep returning to a lesson I learned while reading about the two men on the road to Emmaus. (Luke 24:13-35)

Jesus had just been crucified in Jerusalem and the whole town was talking about it. Two men were walking to Emmaus, which was about seven miles from

Jerusalem, and discussing the recent events. Jesus came up and walked beside them but they were kept from recognizing Him. Jesus asked what the men were discussing and they scoffed and said something to the effect of, "If you have to ask what we're talking about then you're not from around here, are you?!" Jesus talked with them for a long while about many important things, but it wasn't until later that evening when He broke bread with them that their eyes were opened and they realized with whom they had been traveling.

They thought back to their walk, and—here's the important part—remembered, "Were not our hearts burning within us while He was speaking to us on the road, while He was explaining the Scriptures to us?" (Luke 24:32)

I love this story. I love these men. I can imagine the scene when their eyes were opened. In my mind, after they recognize Him, they start elbowing each other with giddy, boyish excitement. Their mouths are agape in wide, bewildered smiles. They razz each other with, "Seeeee??!!" and "I told you!!!"

These men's spirits knew who this stranger was.

He seemed familiar to them yet they overlooked an inner tug.

Slow to believe, Jesus says. (Luke 24:25)

In retrospect, they knew that Jesus had walked alongside them, but at the time? That just wasn't possible! The idea of walking next to Jesus, considering all the facts... it simply didn't make sense. So they didn't consider it.

But sometimes, in the moment, God doesn't make sense.

I wouldn't be surprised if Noah had the same thought. And Moses might have too. And Paul probably did as well. After all, Noah was likely doing just fine before God asked Him to build an ark for all of the wildlife... ever created. And Moses must have thought God was a fool when He had him wander in a desert for 40 long years. And Paul, who probably saw himself filling stadiums and preaching, perhaps suspected things had gone awry when instead of doing that, he was writing letters from prisons. A lot of head scratching and fist shaking, I would imagine. *What are you doing? Why do you have me here? It doesn't make any sense!!*

But God has His own plans about how to start anew, free His people, and get His word out.

And it's not my job to know every detail. It's just my job to listen. Like they did.

I'm no Noah, Moses, or Paul, but maybe I could be. Because sometimes He asks nice guys to build giant vessels. And sometimes He asks the unwilling to lead thousands for decades. And sometimes He asks brilliant men to be in chains. And sometimes He asks non-writers to write. Sometimes He doesn't make sense.

The men on the road to Emmaus taught me not to go around questioning the impractical all the time. They taught me not to skip over what seems ludicrous. They taught me instead to be aware of my heart. Is there a burning? Do I recognize Him in that burning?

Whatever has my heart stirring might be crazy or impossible or impractical or silly, but the only thing that is mine to discern is that burn. The rest is God's. And a good answer, one that makes a little more sense, might come in retrospect.

* * *

We live in Bryan/College Station, Texas, home of Texas A&M University. There is youth everywhere. It's in the tailgating, and by tailgating I mean riding my bumper, not enjoying a football game from the tailgate, although there is that too. It's in the quiet mornings and rowdy nights. It's in all the latest trends walking around town. There is something about this age of human that my personality is drawn to, that my gifts seem aligned to serving.

After praying the prayer, "Here I am. Send me," God has delighted me with a house full of college women to befriend and mentor. Being the person that these girls need me to be at the moment—a listener, a guider, a speaker, a warm house, a loud family, a friend, a gentle reminder, a soft rebuke, someone to sit with, a home cooked meal—whatever it is, it is light and fulfilling.

Through them, I have been reminded that His burden is light. This service, it suits me.

I love these girls. They pile on, and cuddle up, and lean in, and stay too long, and text too late, and need a lot. Then they go about their business, and ignore my text, and show up when I've just lain-down for a nap. They giggle and gossip and make up songs and take endless selfies. Then, the very next moment, they meditate and journal and serve and shock me with weighty wisdom, their truest voice, and a vulnerability that adults seem to have learned to cover up. They handle dramatic, real life circumstances with stoicism, wisdom, and grace, and then think the world is ending when they are stood up or get a lousy group for a group project. They are learners. It takes such humility to have a teachable spirit, and these precious girls know that they do not have all the answers. They are young and they know it. They are not trying to be anything different. And this youth, it makes them tread lightly and hold loosely and seek, seek, seek. What room God has in hearts like that!

I love you, girls. So very much. I love you. And this book is for you.

These pages are simply my stories and how God has revealed Himself to me in them.

I have tried my best to explain how deeply loved you are, how incredibly beautiful you are, how when nothing seems to be making any sense, really we are just waiting to recognize our Lord.

Our circumstances may hurt. We may be lonely. We may rage at the injustices around us. We may have to wait longer than we would care to. Sometimes we walk a long road without seeing Him on it. But He's there. Our eyes will be opened. Just wait.

* * *

Rock Paper Scissors came to me in the middle of the night one night. After a long day banging out a long to-do list, I had trouble sleeping as my mind raced, analyzing which of the day's activities would carry over to the next. Straddling consciousness and sleep, half memory, half dream, I got stuck in a circular game of Rock Paper Scissors with my son. Over and over we went through the motions. I would win and then he would win. The move that worked before would fail the next time. The move that let me down previously would then make me a champion, over and over and over, my son's laughter practically audible. Call it a dream, call it a vision but whatever the case, my son said, "Mommy, I can't decide which weapon I like best. They are all powerful in their own way. Rocks are a strong foundation. Paper is covering what we don't want to see. And Scissors get rid of all the bad stuff."

I had never put any amount of thought into Rock Paper Scissors before. His depth endeared me. I let silence hang in the air between us as I digested what he "said." I was instantly reminded of the Trinity—the Sovereignty of our Lord, the grace of Jesus, and refinement of the Holy Spirit—Rock Paper Scissors. Indeed.

In the writing of this book God has surprised me, taken me down roads I did not know that I wanted to see, comforted me when the process didn't come easily, encouraged me when it didn't go my way, and assured me that His way is always best. By following my stirring heart and not quenching the Holy Spirit with questions, doubt, practicality, reason, or fear, I recognize Him more easily. I am not so slow to believe. Writing as a non-writer taught me to quit telling God about what He made but instead to let Him be the one to tell me a few things.

Because it could happen.

Nothing is impossible.

Just ask Noah, Moses, or Paul.

Just ask the two on the road to Emmaus.

Just ask me.

Following your burning heart, giving the impossible a chance, well, you just might find yourself across a table from Him that way.

INTRODUCTION

"Be strong and courageous, and act; do not fear nor be dismayed, for the Lord God, my God, is with you. He will not fail you nor forsake you until all the work for the service of the house of the Lord is finished." (1 Chronicles 28:20)

To Consider:

1. When you take on a challenge, are you typically optimistic or pessimistic? What are the messages that either spur you on or discourage you?
2. Describe a time that you felt an urgency to do something.
3. Have you ever wondered if you were capable of the desires of your heart?
4. What would you say are your giftings?

To Practice:

Make a list of your goals. Next to each goal provide a reasonable amount of time to accomplish it.

To Listen:

1. "Come on My Soul" by Rend Collective
2. "Set a Fire" by Jesus Culture

ROCK

My firm foundation,
Not moved by wind or my doubt,
Sovereign, Strong, Steady

CHAPTER 1:

Car Keys & Cheap Grace

"I begin by the grass to be bound again by the Lord."
—GEORGE W. RUSSELL (A.E.)

I am a terrible evangelist.

I blame the introverted part of my personality.

When it comes to sharing my faith, I would rather *write* about the Lord and what He has done for me. When nudged by the Holy Spirit to witness to a stranger, I would be glad to *pen* a lengthy discourse about God and His divinity. When confronted by a disbelieving friend, I wouldn't at all mind shooting off an *email* about Jesus and His saving grace. My testimony via *text*? Sounds completely reasonable to me.

Frankly, I am better in writing. Public professions of faith are not exactly my bag.

When convicted to witness face to actual face, I squirm and I stutter and, every time, end up talking about something negligible, like God helping me to find my car keys. I feel so overwhelmed by God's majesty and goodness that when I have an encounter with someone who may want to know more about it, all that majesty and goodness get reduced to me stammering about the Lord delivering me from my disorganization and a terribly bad mood. These trifling tales are what I have to offer. Not the cross. Not Calvary. Not Mary or Joseph or Peter or Paul. Not His love for sinners. Not His perfect life. Not His saving grace. Just me, my lack of order, and Him bailing me out. It's not ideal.

It has potential to go like this:

> *I know that there is a God because He consistently directs me to my car keys just when I am about to have a temper tantrum of epic proportions.*

That's why you are a Christian?

> *Well, yeah, you see, I don't have a key chain. I just carry around a single key for my car and I lose it all the time. And God, He helps me find*

it. I can be cussing and pushing my kids aside, and ransacking junk drawers, but when I finally get my wits about me and think to pray for God to please, for the love of Toyota, help me, I always find it seconds later. Seconds! He comes through every time. Even though I just cussed a blue streak and scared the kids a little.

(Blank stares all around.) (End scene.)

When it comes to telling people who don't know the Lord about what He's done for them, while looking at them in real time, I think dogs howl and babies cry and other believers hide their eyes.

I believe whole-heartedly that there is a God. I do. But to be honest, I can't put my finger squarely on why. This makes me a terrible evangelist. I realize that no one else would hear about my car keys and buy in, but when I try to explain the God in me and my assurance of it... well... I can't.

The concept of an omnipotent God is difficult to grasp, let alone put intelligent words to. It is so vast. I am overwhelmed by all that He is. My car key approach is just that simple because it is just that complicated.

And speaking of complicated, I was looking at my deodorant the other day and right there on the side, it said that it works with my body's natural chemistry. How in the world does it do that, I wondered?! I shrugged my shoulders and put it on. I don't understand electricity either but that doesn't keep me from using the heck out of it. There are things that are confounding. What my microwave does, the speed of light, photosynthesis, ice melting. I'm just kidding, I get that last one.

I can't make sense of all of the details of God but I know, with awestruck wonder, the feeling that has captured my heart.

God is majestic. God is grandiose. God is magnificent. Pardon me for being made speechless. How do you put awestruck wonder into words?

One of the best books I have ever read about the Bible is *The Stranger on the Road to Emmaus* by John Cross. In it, he so logically tells of the whole Bible's themes, weaving them together, binding the Bible's entire text into one cohesive drama-filled story. It is masterful. Even though I had been going to church for fifteen years before I read it, it was in its pages that I gained a more thorough, detailed, and chronological understanding of the Book on which I had based my life. Cross begins his book by analyzing the perplexing nature of God.

On the first day, God simply spoke light and dark into place. On the second day, He created the sky. On the third day, God created land and covered it in plants and vegetation. On the fourth day, He made the light givers, the sun and the moon, and all of the heavenly bodies.

On the fifth day, God made sea life and birds. The sixth day was God's pinnacle as He created land animals and man. And on the seventh day, He rested, but not because He was tired, just to relish in all that He called good. (Genesis 1:1-2:3)

Because the Bible is full of understatements, greatness can be skimmed over. It is tempting to read about creation and then move on to Philippians. But wait. He *spoke* things into place. Just *spoke* some galaxies into existence. It sounds inconceivable, doesn't it?

Do you know what else sounds inconceivable? The very universe that He created.

Cross outlines in his book the amazing statistics of our solar system and uses them to prove that God's eternal existence is vast, but vast does not mean impossible. While reading his words and appreciating his examples I realized that it is true that filing something away as "totally, completely, one hundred percent *amazing* but totally, completely, one hundred percent *true*" is actually something that we are quite used to.

For example, I learned that if we were to travel at the speed of light we would circle the earth seven and a half times in one second. Seven times. And a half! One second! At the speed of light it would take two whole seconds to pass the moon. Two seconds! Just to get to the moon. I am bad at math (I really think it should solve its own problems) so forgive me for asking, "Did you catch that?" In *one* second we circled the Earth *seven* times, but in two seconds we just went to the moon. It gets better. It would take four whole minutes at the speed of light to get to Mars, which is our closest planet. Pluto? Five hours! And that's just our solar system, which is a tiny dot on a map of galaxies! At the speed of light, the next closest galaxy is 2,000,000 years away.

Isn't that crazy?! Doesn't that seem impossible?! But do you believe it? Totally, completely, one hundred percent *amazing* but totally, completely, one hundred percent *true*.

Electricity seems impossible and I know for certain that it works. My deodorant seems impossible and it impresses me every single day. The universe seems impossible but I believe with certainty that what Scientists tell me is true. So how could I deny my very own heart and what I know deep inside just because I am not able to tell of it neatly?

Don't we want an impossible God? *I want an impossible God!*

Because we can't get our minds around Him is a terrible reason to dismiss Him.

Do we dismiss the universe because it is astonishing?

Would He not being indescribable make Him easier to believe in?

If He were less?

If He were more like us?

God is difficult to grasp. A God who knows everything, is all powerful, can be everywhere at once, is difficult for us to grasp. But so is our universe! So is my deodorant! All of them are mind-boggling. All of them are real. And we have been invited to share in the majesty of it all.

* * *

Jesus tells us about our invitation to His Kingdom in the shocking Parable of the King and the Marriage Feast. (Matthew 22:1-14) In this story, the King invited his guests to his son's marriage, but they would not come. He invited them again, letting them know of all that awaited them once they arrived, the very best that he had to offer, yet again they "made light of it and went off, one to his farm, another to his business." (Matthew 22:5)

Some of the people did more than ignore the invitation; they actually killed the couriers! So the King became angry and he burned their city and destroyed the murderers, deeming the invited guests unworthy. He then invited those off the streets instead, anyone and everyone, the good and the bad, all were welcome now!

The wedding hall was full and the King was finally hosting the celebration for which he was longing. But as the King looked around, he noticed that someone had snuck in without the required wedding robe. The King kindly asked the robeless guest for an explanation, but he had no answer. So the King had him cast out into the outer darkness where there was weeping and gnashing of teeth.

Sheesh. Who needs HBO? This is intense!

This narrative is a tool to get our attention, to take us by the shoulders and give us a shake. Jesus' audience apparently needed a shake.

The symbolism of this parable is straightforward, and speaks plainly to the fact that we have been specifically invited to a feast (an invitation to God's kingdom), by the most important person in the land (God), for the most honorable of guests (His Son), for the most important event ever (uniting humanity with God). The best of food, the best of venues, the best of company! Embossed with our names, that invitation He delivered is specifically ours.

To put the egregiousness of the King's people in perspective, let us imagine being personally invited by the President to attend a sacred event and responding by saying that we had to check our calendars, or, even more egregious, killing the person who sent us the message!

This is a preposterous response! It is inconceivable to tell the King of our land that we will pencil him in. The subjects' response is evidence of their underestimation of the King's importance and overestimation of their own. The bottom line of this parable is that the King's people openly refused to give him the honor that he was due. The King, so worthy of praise, was reaching out in selfless and surprising generosity, but his gesture failed to capture their attention. He couldn't even get their attention. It is not like they dismissed him to wallow in a den of sin instead. They simply had some work to do, life to attend to.

But it gets better.

As Flannery O'Connor says, "in a land of the deaf you have to shout." Jesus is certainly shouting when He warns His audience about approaching the wedding feast and not donning a wedding garment.

Not only did the King want his people to respond, but also he desperately wanted them to put on what he offered. Long and white, the wedding garment served as an outward sign to the believer's inner assent.

The King desperately wanted his guests to share in the joy of his kingdom. His anger was evidence of his desire to share his majesty with his guests if only they would have come, honored his son, shed their own clothes, and taken what was his.

* * *

Jesus taught in many different areas to many different audiences. He taught in people's homes, by the sea, at the well, and in the temple to Jews and Gentiles, men and women, religious leaders and lay people; simply no one was excluded from the proclamation of the gospel.

The day that Jesus taught using the parable of the King and his son's wedding banquet, He was in the temple and there was a large crowd including many religious leaders, the Pharisees and the Sadducees, who hated Jesus for His counter cultural ways and merciful messages. The Pharisees and the Sadducees, in an effort to please God, became so obsessed with laws that they had long forgotten the one thing God really wanted was a relationship.

Certainly, in Jesus' storytelling, this parable struck a chord with the religious leaders, for they were proud of their invitation but rejected the One who went along with it and insisted on their own merit and their own dirty clothes, as if they were the ones doing the inviting and gift giving. They saw themselves in His story. Jesus and the Pharisees? They were communicating just fine.

And I know that I am like those Pharisees because this story is meant for me. It is tempting to distance myself from the people who hated Jesus and align myself with his disciples instead. But I can't get the most out of His messages if I don't ask myself the hard questions. How do I make light of my invitation? How have I failed to give Him my attention? Have I rejected the wedding garment?

No thanks, I say. *That's okay*, I reply. *I've got this*, I insist. *Don't get me wrong, I'm glad I'm here, but I don't so much like that robe. I'll keep mine. Thanks.* All the while denying Jesus and the power of that garment.

An appallingly inaccurate power shift, one removing God of power and employing ourselves instead, has allowed us to make decisions that are not ours to make. We take it upon ourselves to decide which rules matter and which rules really don't. We have underestimated the King's importance and overestimated our own. We have forgotten how awesome and worthy of wonder He is.

Frankly we have forgotten whom we are dealing with.

God has given us grace. That is true. He has poured it on lavishly. Undeserved and unmerited, He longs for us to find a place at His table, to accept His invitation, for He takes great delight in us. But we must not confuse kindness with weakness.

In reality, the same breath used to pardon our sins, could also send the mountains crumbling into the sea.

He has given us grace.

He has invited us to His fancy feast.

But we should not walk in nonchalantly and deny a wedding robe.

When we ignore the character of God and make light of His invitation, it wipes out reverence, and allows us easily, without conviction, to do what *we* want. When we acknowledge the power and generosity of God and understand what our invitation entails, it moves us lovingly, with transformation, to do what *He* wants.

I still have so much to learn, but after recognizing whom I am dealing with, accepting my invitation, and donning that robe, I have committed to practicing gratefulness as a good place to start my journey through His banquet hall. We have to start somewhere and as I look around at what has been prepared for me, gratefulness seems appropriate. Simply noticing miracles that capture my mind, my eye, and my heart and giving Him glory has allowed me to catch God doing what He does so well—loving me. Simple treasures and small miracles abound when I see Him in the moment. Favors with my name on them. Blessings folded up and slipped in my pocket. Missing car keys, instantly found. I have insisted on leaving a world where an invitation from a King is dismissed, and have embraced a world where God is everywhere and I pay tribute by simply noticing. Awed adoration. Great reverence and thanks. It is a grand party indeed.

I remember being twenty-four, young and on my own, in a faraway country with three of my very best girlfriends. It was late at night and we were in the middle of the jungle in a canoe snaking down a river with what must have been one jillion trillion stars in the sky like pinholes above us. The trees hung low and the air smelled foreign. We giggled with our tour guide trying to understand one another without a common language, relying on charades. We laughed and laughed that night in the middle of the jungle. I was on an adventure thick with His breathtaking creation and was overwhelmed by His kindness that He allowed me this night to laugh in a canoe with people I treasured. In the privacy of our midnight setting, I lifted my hands up to that starry sky and whispered thank you.

I also remember being in labor. I was induced with Pitocin but didn't have pain medication and the contractions weren't natural contractions. They were more violent, closer together, and the delivery was all together more intense than anyone expected—especially me. My husband wrapped himself around me and did nothing but fight that fight with me. I felt his tears on my face as he struggled right along with me as if our pain were shared. I'm not sure that it wasn't. And then. Quickly, so quickly. There she was. A little girl. She came out puffy from all the work that she and I had already done together. I was amazed by all that we had already accomplished, she and I. And I had no words. I couldn't get any words out. And yet, I have never felt more fully alive in my whole life.

You don't have to be bringing life into the world or in a foreign country to feel pure reverent wonder. The day-to-day ordinary moments can be just as awesome. I remember one Sunday after church sitting in a Mexican restaurant with a best friend and her husband. It was a Sunday where all the stars aligned and all six of our children behaved in church. We were celebrating and talking on a festive patio. Our kids were on the playground and throughout our soulful conversation, we got to watch them play. From our seats, we could feel the sunshine and hear our kids' laughter. There was Mariachi music playing. And there I was, discussing important things with my husband whom I adore, my dearest friend for whom I would take a bullet, and her husband who is pure gold. Everything was just right in its place. And I was totally overwhelmed with the rightness of it all.

When we respond to our own personal invitation and become aware of what has been given, we can't help but be awed by Him. And with good reason! There is so much to be taken by when we open our hearts to all that He has prepared for us, for the lengths that He has gone to entertain us, to capture us! Animals, music, nature, friendships, babies, our bodies, science, art, and on and on and on. This world that He has given us is full of His beauty and when we show up grateful for our invitation, cloaked in the most generous of gifts, we start to give Him some of the credit He deserves. No more denying invitations. No more showing up nonchalant and unimpressed. No more calling our own shots.

Jesus' audience still needs that shake.

I can't help but wonder if the King's subjects didn't celebrate their invitation because they found it unbelievable.

Did they think of their King as removed, distant, and unengaged?

To them, was he a mythical being, too concerned with his own affairs to care about the details of theirs?

Perhaps their invitation was easy to dismiss because it was outlandish. *This is an invitation from the King? For me? To his castle? To celebrate something sacred? Right. Hey, I've got a deadline to meet at work, but that was a good one!*

Maybe they just simply didn't believe that to be true. It was too unfathomable, too unlikely. The idea of a powerful yet benevolent King is indeed astounding.

But couldn't they look at the roads he recently had paved for their convenience? Or his army at work for the safety of his people? Instead of disbelief, couldn't they choose to simply look around and be grateful?

Couldn't they commit to curiosity instead of indifference and then see proof of his power?

The idea of a powerful yet benevolent King is astounding. That is true. And the idea of Him wanting to commune with us is even more astounding. That is also true.

But being astonished by the invitation is a terrible reason to dismiss it.

His greatness should never be the barrier to an amazing celebration!

I want an impossible King.

The universe and the speed of light and my deodorant have taught me that impossibility is a great delight and this parable has taught me that dismissing it is costly.

* * *

As I was writing this chapter, my husband, after taking out the trash, came inside talking about the stars. He was overwhelmed by them this night in particular. "There are stars between the stars," he said. We used to live in the country and didn't take for granted the beauty of a clear night. As he was talking, somewhat to himself, definitely in awe, he went on a tangent about the North Star, a star that has guided sojourners for centuries. "If you only know that one detail, the rest of your travels fall into place," he mumbled. I smiled at his wonder, endeared by his thankful heart.

The more he talked about the North Star guiding its followers, the more I thought of our Lord. Knowing that He is King is all we really need to know. Keeping Him in His proper place, due North, and letting everything else happen as a consequence of that one detail might seem a little crazy in a world where a computer can comment on our journey every 1/4 of a mile, directing our every veer, telling us our missed turns, and always rerouting, rerouting, rerouting.

I pondered on the majesty of just one Director, one Light, one Source—the kindness of the simplicity, the bravery to trust. What the shepherds and wise men followed to find their King is a wonderful metaphor for the rest of us navigating our own uncertain paths. We are to keep our eye on the prize, place one foot in front of the other, not aware of every detail, unsure of the twists and turns, but certain of the reference point, a guiding light.

I was writing about sovereignty and I couldn't think of anything more sovereign than One light guiding us home. I googled the North Star to learn a few things thinking that perhaps I could include what I learned here in these pages. I henpecked "North Star." Pushed enter. And the first thing I read told me that the North Star is actually a triple star system.

My mouth fell open, and my eyes teared up.

And that's it.

That right there.

That's how I know that there is a God.

It's a little better than finding my car keys, and holds a little more wonder than Mariachi music, but it's all the same. Gratitude for the invitation. Curiosity to look around. Reverence for what I find and knowing for certain that what's there is from Him.

And all of it is hard to explain isn't it?

That feeling of gratitude and amazement when my husband walks through the door having found a simple pleasure while doing a menial chore, inspiring me to do the same, and the Lord saying, "Thanks for noticing but I've got more. That star you likened me to? Look. It's a Trinity."

I cry a little for the gift. For the amazing gift of knowing Him with certainty.

Yes, it's hard to put into words, but all of a sudden stammering and stuttering and mumbling and bumbling seems appropriate. God is majestic. God is grandiose. God is magnificent. Pardon me for being made speechless. How do you put awestruck wonder into words?

"The heavens are telling of the glory of God; And their expanse is declaring the work of His hands. Day to day pours forth speech, And night to night reveals knowledge. There is no speech, nor are there words; Their voice is not heard." (Psalm 19:1)

To Consider:

1. If you are a believer, how easy is it for you to share your faith? If you are not a believer, what would be refreshing to hear in regard to someone else's faith?
2. Is the size or goodness of God an obstacle to believing in Him fully? Have you ever felt like perhaps you believe in something too outlandish to be true? If you are not a believer, what are other obstacles besides God being outlandish? Do you believe that God can handle doubt?
3. Does what you believe about God line up with what the Word tells us about His character?
4. How does nonchalance, arrogance, or independence affect disbelief?

To Practice:

For one month, write down the little things that grab your attention and make you feel thankful.

To Listen:

1. "Love Song for a Savior" by Jars of Clay
2. "King of Love" by I Am They

CHAPTER 2:

Dirty Diaper Gospel

"The quality of mercy is not strain'd,
It droppeth as the gentle rain from heaven
Upon the place beneath: it is twice blest;
It blesseth him that gives and him that takes:
'Tis mightiest in the mightiest: it becomes
The throned monarch better than his crown;
His sceptre shows the force of temporal power,
The attribute to awe and majesty,
Wherein doth sit the dread and fear of kings;
But mercy is above this sceptred sway;
It is enthroned in the hearts of kings,
It is an attribute to God himself;
And earthly power doth then show likest God's
When mercy seasons justice."

—WILLIAM SHAKESPEARE

I was watching my kids at soccer one night a couple of years ago. It was such a glorious mess.

My son and my daughter played at the same time on neighboring fields and it was all my pleasure watching them exert themselves physically by picking flowers on a soccer field. My son was four so there was a little more discipline in his class than in my two year old daughter's class, but only barely.

In my daughter's class, the coach arranged a little game where everyone had a scarf tucked into the back of their shorts and they all ran around chasing each other while trying to grab each other's scarves. My daughter got a purple one, which was her current favorite color. She really liked it, so instead of chasing the other kids, she sat down with her scarf, fashioned it into a bonnet and sang a show tune in the middle of the field. She didn't want anyone else's scarf, she just wanted to twirl in hers.

In my son's class, the coach was trying to get the kids to use the insides of their feet to learn to dribble the ball. This is best explained as walking like a duck, so the kids made a line and duck-walked trying their best to keep a soccer ball between their feet while waddling, quacking, and flapping their little wings. My son knows when things are silly and doesn't always enjoy being an adult's punch line. So when he just sat down in the middle of the field while everyone else walked around duck-like, I asked him what was wrong. He responded that if he had to be a duck, he would rather just sit on his eggs right now.

It's beautiful really, all the kids doing their own thing, breaking all the rules as they go, sometimes forgetting the most fundamental rule of soccer, and instead picking up the ball, tucking it under their arm, and running with it like they are sprinting for the end zone, the wrong game completely.

I looked around that night at all the spectators and everyone was having the time of their lives watching these little people perfectly ruin the game of soccer. It was wonderful.

That night as I loaded them in the car, giddy with love for these precious people the Lord has let me babysit for Him, I smelled something awful. It was my daughter. The details aren't necessary but the diaper that she had produced was a family record. There was no waiting until we got home. This was a category five, code brown. We drove a minivan at the time so I laid her in the back and did what I had to do. Because soccer nights are a bit hectic, I long forgot about the diaper in the back as I unloaded the car. The next day, Friday, was a day the babies did not go to school and they didn't have school again until Tuesday. Point being, for four whole days a mammoth poopy diaper baked in the back of our car in the Texas May sun.

Ready for school on Tuesday, we opened the passenger door to the minivan to pile in and almost passed out. The second we opened the door we were met by a heavy fog of putrid stench. It was unbearable. It was revolting. It was wretched. It was tempting just to stay home. Calling in sick would have only barely been an exaggeration. It was so foul that I think we held our collective breath for the seven minutes that it took us to drive to school.

I had long forgotten about the diaper and could not for the life of me find the offensive source, surely something dead, that was polluting our car. I searched and searched, walking away to breathe heavily, taking breaks, gasping for fresh air. I literally could not stand it. We avoided unnecessary trips in the car. My husband and I took his car for errands. We rearranged a couple of car seats so I could take the kids to school in his car. For two more days, our minivan was useless as it sat in our driveway, taking up space, stinking to high heaven.

Finally, my son, who was certainly complaining the loudest, said that he thought he saw something under his seat. I instantly remembered the diaper. I grabbed a jillion plastic grocery bags, scooped it up while the kids chanted for me, put it in the outside trash, and promptly put the trash can on the curb even though trash day wasn't for another two days.

* * *

In Genesis, we are introduced to the Bible's main characters: God and man. We learn of God's perfect creation and the pieces of beauty it contains. In our sinful, fallen world, it might be hard to imagine perfection because we simply don't know what we don't know. Imagining a garden where rain isn't necessary because water springs up from the ground is quite a stretch. Imagining a place where God took evening strolls with us is unfathomable. Imagining nakedness without unease or discomfort or shame is unthinkable. Aside from these small details, we don't know much about the Garden of Eden except that God called it very good and due to His holy nature, He could not create anything less than perfection.

God gave Adam and Eve love and friendship. Adam and Eve obeyed and honored Him in return.

That was the deal. Everyone agreed. Everything was perfect.

Until...

Adam and Eve had free will, but free will is just a notion without options. Obeying when there are not choices is a meaningless obedience. So God gave Adam and Eve an alternative. Their obedience needed to be true.

There was the Tree of Life. If you ate from it, you lived forever. But the second tree came with a warning. It was the Tree of the Knowledge of Good and Evil and if you ate from it, you died. This restriction presented Adam and Eve with a choice.

Satan, a vengeful angel, fighting for God's greatest creation, slithered into the garden to do what he does best. He didn't announce his presence with flashing lights or neon signs. He didn't march in blaring what he was there to accomplish. That's not the way Satan works, for no good-intentioned lover of God would follow him that way. Instead, with all the subtlety and deception that he could muster, he casually asked a question. Just one tiny, mocking question. I can almost hear his hissing condescension.

"'[H]as God said, "You shall not eat from any tree of the garden"?' For God knows that in the day you eat from it your eyes will be opened, and you will be like God, knowing good and evil." (Genesis 3:1,5)

That's what Satan does. Sneaky and deceitful. Nuanced and cunning. He entices us into thinking that we can be our own God, decide what is best for us, suit ourselves. He convinced Eve with half-truths that perhaps God did not really care as much as He claimed to, that God was probably holding out on her. *Did God really say that?* Suddenly, the rest of the garden simply wasn't enough. Desiring more, Adam and Eve ate the fruit.

What happened after is what always happens when laws are broken—there are consequences. For a brief moment, Adam and Eve abandoned their relationship with God. They left the comfort of paradise to flirt with a forbidden alternative and when they did, their greed and suspicion severed their bond with God because a perfect God cannot allow fickle friendships or slight betrayals. Their communion was over. His perfection could no longer be with this imperfection.

Perfection was ruined by disobedience. And the penalty was death. The rules were never unclear.

I'm going to be honest. In my Christian faith, I have struggled with original sin. The fall has been hard for me. Eating an apple seems like a trivial offense for such grave consequences. Curiosity seems like a terrible reason to call the whole thing off. What I understand now is that I didn't appreciate the magnificence of God or the simple truth that His perfection simply could not allow imperfection.

Around the time that a diaper was baking in our minivan, I was reading John Cross's previously mentioned *Stranger on the Road to Emmaus*. In it, Cross likens humanity's sin to a dead animal under the hut he was staying in while serving abroad. The stench was intolerable, making the hut untenable. They were simply going to have to move, it was that bad. With his written example and the one baking in my backseat, I finally was able to put sin into perspective.

The legendary dirty diaper that turned our family upside down for almost a week told me something about my God and my disobedience. It was through poop that I could better understand how God feels about sin and the severity of it.

That diaper was unbearable.

I wasn't avoiding it because I was histrionic, harsh, or overly sensitive.

I was avoiding it because it was unnatural for me to share space with it.

I needed out of its presence.

I wasn't angry or ill-tempered.

I was just doing what my nature had me do.

Cross says our sin is a stench in His perfect nostrils and it separates us from Him.

Just like I needed that diaper wrapped up and placed as far away from our home as possible, so God has had to remove Himself from us. It doesn't mean that He is pleased about it. This isn't a haughty, punishing separation. It is quite the opposite. He is devastated by it. How grieved He must have been to have His creation ravaged and our relationship hindered. But the rules were never unclear. Holiness demands the absence of sin. A perfect God cannot allow it in His presence. It is not natural.

When Adam and Eve disobeyed, a law had been broken. So a sentence was given. Our God is a just God. We were debtors, it was now our condition, and we had a price to pay.

But God longs to be with us. Made in His image, the pinnacle of His creation, God yearns to stroll with us once more. Angry at the one who deceived us and pained that we were duped, as just as our God is, He is equally loving.

So He came up with a solution.

This is a little embarrassing to write out loud, but it's the truth so I'll risk it. The Bible can be difficult for me. Not only are there many things in it that make me want to kick something, but for someone who loves words, too much information, and over-sharing in general, I oftentimes find the Bible to be a little... well... vague. I feel like you aren't supposed to write these things out loud. I'm feeling regretful already.

But!

Every now and then, when I really put my soul into understanding something, a powerful prayer experience courtesy of the Holy Spirit, will make something that was once flat a little more three-dimensional.

I'll show you what I mean.

I mentioned my trouble with the fall. Because I can be a shortsighted brat, my tendency is to think that God is a big ol' meanie for freaking out about an apple. But then, in an effort to understand Him better, I settle into my couch, close my eyes, and put myself in the middle of that beautiful garden where neon colors, fragrant flowers, and friendly animals delight my senses and my soul. I contemplate His beautiful creation. I meditate on what He called good. I ponder His foreign divinity. How big He is. How small I am. What I know He knows. What I think I know. And the difference in between. I examine what I know of His best-laid plans and how they were desolated in one greedy moment. I consider how that must have felt. For everyone. I concentrate on those emotions. And I can't help it, but a very, very low budget movie with an elementary script comes to mind, as I ponder what all involved in the fall must have been thinking. With cardboard props and cheesy costumes, the setting is my junior high cafeteria. It goes something like this:

> **Adam**: *God. This is terrible. We feel terrible. Everything is all wrong now. What can we do?*

> **God**: *The damage has been done. The penalty is death. Adam. Eve. You always knew the rules. This is the law.*

> **Eve**: *Can we have mercy? Isn't mercy also a law?*

> **God**: *But then there wouldn't be justice. Do you see? I am holy. I insist on justice. Mercy cannot rob justice.*

> **Adam**: *But if you do not forgive our debt, then there won't be mercy.*

> **God**: *Right. Do you see the mess you have made? It's a problem, isn't it? I need justice. You need mercy. Neither prevails except at the cost of the other, it seems.*

Eve: *God. Could both laws ever be served?*

God: *Well. Yes. But it is going to take Someone else. And it is deeply painful.*

(Enter Jesus, stage right.)

Jesus: *Father, I would like to accept punishment for these kind friends. They have made a foolish mistake. They know not what they have done. They are unable to give You what You deserve, but I can't stand to see them die because of it. I would like to fulfill the law for them. I can give You what You deserve. This way, You will have been paid justly and mercy will be given. And. Both. I can do it. Will you let me do it?*

God: *This is not easy.*

Jesus to Adam and Eve: *So here's how this works. I am paying your price, people. Do you accept me as your payment? Are we all on the same page here?*

Adam and Eve: *Yes! Please! You have saved us!*

Jesus: *It is finished.*

Perhaps sometimes pretending to eavesdrop on God can shed some light on the complicated things that plague my heart—like the belief that I serve a cantankerous, vicious God when nothing could be further from the truth. When I lean into something that frustrates me instead of turning away with the jerk of a knee, I can usually, almost always, in the comfort of my couch, snuggled up with my Comforter, reach a greater truth.

God is not tapping his haughty toe from on high with his disappointed hands on his holy hips. God is not taking pleasure in our distance. He has gone to very great lengths to rectify what was ruined.

God sent Jesus to be everything that we couldn't be. And Jesus walked down from heaven and involved Himself in our sinful lives in the most intimate of ways. His hands dirty and His heart broken, Jesus took it on. He braved our sin and paid the price. And because of that, God's great holiness can only be rivaled by His great love.

On the cross, we find the perfectly balanced expression of BOTH attributes—infinite in both physical directions, extending, ever extending, both ways, the cross our eternal solution, justice satisfied, mercy administered.

This is the Good News.

* * *

Many years ago, after an exhausting day of teaching young people with special needs, I came home and googled "I hate my job. If I have to go one more day, I think I might die. I really love animals but I don't want to be a vet. I think animals help people heal. I want to facilitate that. Help me, Google. I mean, God." Shockingly, I found a master's program that promised to teach me how to train dogs for people with disabilities. I called right away.

I enrolled in the program and, for the first time, excelled as a student. Classes that I had historically struggled with like Biology and Statistics came with ease. I had a way with the animals—which I always knew about myself—but aside from collecting dog hair at my friends' houses because their animals were drawn to me, becoming increasingly unpopular with my family for bringing home stray after stray, and enjoying a children's petting zoo way more than a grown woman should, it was a skill that had never actually come in handy. Even though I was one of the few students with no previous experience, I was chosen by my peers to represent our class with commencement speeches at both of our graduations. I felt like I finally found something I was good at. This work, it suited me.

I also felt deeply that the work mattered. People with disabilities were in many ways being freed by their new dog companion. Mobility, confidence, support, friendship—these people's lives were changed by a dog that I trained. It was a rich time in my life.

When my husband and I moved to our new community, I decided to take my skills into animal shelters, the local jail, and nursing homes. They all went together perfectly in my mind. My idea took a little convincing (this was before every jail had therapy dogs and a show on *Bravo*), but I was persistent. I visited jails and nursing homes and explained that I would temperament-test shelter dogs to see if they would be candidates for a training program. I would take the chosen dogs into the jail. I would match them with a detainee and I would teach classes to teach the detainee how to train their dog. Then, at the end of our program, they, as a team, would go into nursing homes to provide social therapy.

It would be beautiful!

You can imagine the obstacles. *You want to bring a stray dog and a convicted felon into our nursing home with possibly the most vulnerable population in the community?* I begged people not to hang up on me. Shockingly, a few of them didn't.

It truly was beautiful.

The participating dogs benefitted because, through training, we actually solved some of the issues that had them in the shelter in the first place. There were waiting lists ten people deep to adopt one of our dogs.

The benefits for the detainees in the program were innumerable. Mastering the emotional regulation that training a dog required had potential to be life-changing.

One of the very first lessons we learned in class was that adult wolves don't bark. If they do, it is usually in a state of fear. Barking is reserved for wolf cubs or fearful adults. However, unlike canines, primates do bark. In fact, primates tend to follow the guy who can make the most noise. That's quite a difference—adult wolves are quiet, adult humans are noisy. Here was the lesson: Loud noises can gain a dog's attention, but they do not gain a dog's respect. Losing one's cool is not seen as dominant or impressive. It is seen as childish or weak. The qualities that a dog looks for in a leader are calmness, coolness, and centeredness. It is only steady emotions that are effective.

Our wild emotions shut dogs down. Bad tempers, intimidating postures, threatening voices—they simply don't work. In this way, dogs demand our best. It is said that only three emotions are allowed in dog training: happy, happier, and happiest. If only calm happiness works, when a bad mood or frustration sets in, then it's probably time to take a break, go for a short walk, play a little, and sing a catchy song. It's time to change locations, smile at each other, change the tone, and in a minute, try again, but this time a little happier.

Very little of what was happening in our training room week after week was about dog training.

Because, what happens when you take the skill to manage situations with your own emotions into your work place? Into your home? Into a traffic jam? Into an argument? What happens when you recognize your own power to create calmness in order to get what you need?

Peace happens.

I believed in this. And I had reason to: it was working.

These men and women identified with the dog's life of hard knocks. It reached something inside of them, and their relationship with their dog provided a risk-free place to try out the soft underbelly of their vulnerability and goodness.

I keep memories as treasures safe and sound in the space of my heart, and some of my fondest moments were watching grown men covered in scars and tattoos use a dog voice and turn into mush when their buddy wagged into the room. So many individual memories like Craig, who cradled a dog's head, stared deep into his eyes, and apologized over and over from down deep for some minor indiscretion. *I would never hurt ya, Buddy. I would never hurt ya, Buddy.* I waited for the right time and enough rapport to ask with as much love as I could, "I see you. I see your softness. I see your kindness. It is there. And it is good. Now, tell me. Can you apologize to your wife that way?" And then watching the tears come.

Moments like these, they were not an exception. They were a rule. And I wrote and I wrote and I wrote desperate never to forget. Rough men and bad-tempered women healed for short moments at a time while they nurtured and served and took care of their neighbor just like they were designed to do. They just needed time and space to remember. They were remembering. I know that it was so. I saw it.

And the community did too. There were write-ups in the paper and segments on the news. We had demonstrations for people who wanted to give us money.

Our efforts were supported. Our participation was growing. And why? Because it all just made sense! It made sense because the community was interested in kinder neighbors! It was that simple. The community was rejoicing. People were pleased.

But.

Mercy isn't always welcomed. Not by everyone. If the life of Jesus taught us anything at all, it is that grace isn't always celebrated.

We certainly had skeptics.

When they were trying to be polite they would ask me, "Do you really think this program is changing who they are?" Of course, I could never answer that. I could never assume something so bold. I understood better than anyone that I had a very... um... *captive* audience, without the pressure of peers or the lure of illicit substances. I knew that. So I could only answer to what I knew for certain and that was when they were with me, and with their dog, and at the nursing homes, yes, absolutely, for moments, they were changed. And who knew? Maybe with more moments they could see what kindness offered? Maybe kindness was like a muscle and it just needed to be strengthened? And used. Again and again. Stronger and stronger. Until it didn't hurt anymore. Who knew?

When those skeptics weren't trying to be polite, they just put it plainly: "You are coddling criminals."

And maybe that was true.

Every personality test I have ever taken has told me that when it comes to social justice, I am part Care Bear. For better or worse, our proclivities are what they are. I lean the way I lean, and I try to be Godly about it while I look for the God in those leaning the other way. After all, we are all made in the image of the same God. I fight for mercy as an elbow, but my sister fights for justice as a knee, and together, working in unity, we could do brilliant things if we started celebrating different Body parts and quit insisting on sameness.

Knowing that only Jesus was able perfectly to balance justice and mercy allowed me not to be hurt when those criticisms publicly came.

One program could never be the whole Body. One program could never do what the cross did. One program could never perfectly balance justice and mercy. I would never hold those answers. Only Jesus could.

But I felt that those people criticizing the program, in their chase for retribution, had comfortably exalted themselves above others and this seemed to me an ungodly quest for justice, not a righteous one.

Jesus speaks to this very point in His Parable of the Pharisee and the Tax Collector. (Luke 18:9-14) In this story, two men go to the temple to pray, one a Pharisee, the other a tax collector. The Pharisee, standing alone, prayed to God and listed his many righteous deeds. Then he thanked God for not making him like other people, and he rattled off a lengthy list of those whom he considered beneath him.

Included in his list of "others" was the tax collector who was standing far off without even the assumption to turn his eyes to heaven. And unlike the Pharisee, the tax collector beat his breast acknowledging his sin and begged for God's mercy. Jesus tells us that the tax collector "went to his house justified rather than the other; for everyone who exalts himself will be humbled, but he who humbles himself will be exalted." (Luke 18:14)

Through this parable, Jesus shows us that mercy isn't always on the side of the people who most expect it.

The detainees I worked with expected nothing.

In my Church, one of the most beautiful things that I think we do together is pray a prayer of confession. "I confess to Almighty God, and to you my brothers and sisters, that I have sinned through my own fault, in my thoughts and in my words, in what I have done and in what I have failed to do." We stand together. We ask for prayers. We admit our weakness. And while we do it, we pound our chest like this tax collector. With a closed fist over an open heart, we beat three times to remind ourselves of our frailty and need for God. There is no fasting or tithing that suffices for the mercy of our Lord. No righteous deed. Our justification has nothing to do with us. And we pound to remember.

I watch my little girl become a Disney Princess on the soccer field instead of following the rules, and my heart leaps for her. I watch my son rebel and twist the rules to suit himself, and I chuckle at his obstinateness. I watch both of my children make a royal mess of the game of soccer, but to me they are so holy, so dearly loved. I watch them with grace and compassion and I hope with all of my heart that they will turn to me for the wisdom they need before silly mistakes turn into dangerous ones. Right now, in these moments, with them turning to me again and again, mistakes are just an opportunity for my love to abound. When it comes to my children, love is just what I am. As a parent, I pour out grace without even thinking about it. How completely must God cover us in grace if simple, human love is this merciful?

A dirty diaper taught me about God's sovereignty and need for justice, but my kids' soccer game and a few convicts taught me about His love and mercy. Redeemed for knowing we need mercy. Justified by accepting His perfect payment. And. Both. Opposite directions, extending eternal, the cross.

We give it our all and mess up and pound our chests to ask for mercy. We humble ourselves to be exalted, aware that we can't do anything to save ourselves. We are thankful for the Savior who paid and made everything right, restoring us once more.

"He has told you, O man, what is good; And what does the Lord require of you But to do justice, to love kindness, And to walk humbly with your God?" (Micah 6:8)

"The Lord is gracious and merciful; Slow to anger and great in lovingkindness. The Lord is good to all, And His mercies are over all His works." (Psalm 145:8-9)

TO CONSIDER:

1. Have you spent time pondering creation? What about it is surprising/intriguing/confusing?
2. How has your understanding of sin affected your walk? How does your understanding of sin differ from God's?
3. When something about God or Christianity frustrates you, what is your response? Do you turn away or lean in?
4. Do you naturally lean more toward justice or mercy? Is it difficult to understand a God who perfectly delivers both?

TO PRACTICE:

Think of a population who has historically been on the receiving end of your judgment and do one kind thing for them.

TO LISTEN:

1. "Jesus, My Everything" by Matt Maher
2. "How Deep the Father's Love For Us" by Kendall Payne

CHAPTER 3:

Love Smells Like Roast Not Roses

"I have found the paradox, that if you love until it hurts,
there can be no more hurt, only more love."
—MOTHER TERESA

I am not cynical about Valentine's Day. That sounds like an opener about how awful Valentine's Day is from someone who is in fact very cynical about Valentine's Day.

But, honest, I'm not. I am not bitter about mushy love. I happen to love my husband in a mushy way. I do not roll my eyes at what is written on Valentine's Day cards. Well, maybe sometimes, but it is not because I don't agree with it. Sweet, chalky candy with written messages on it? Please! I think that's awesome. A heart? My favorite shape. I am not the least bit stubborn about being romantic on command and the commercial spectacle of red and pink doesn't bother me. I am not cynical about Valentine's Day.

There's a "but" coming. Can you hear it?

I guess the reason that Valentine's Day gets a shrug and a "meh" from me is not because I fundamentally disagree with it, but because I think it leaves out too many details and covers up too many truths. I am convinced that covering something up is the same thing as lying and has the same effect on our spirit. After all, admit it, how many fights have happened on Valentine's Day because it was Valentine's Day? I'm just a stickler for the truth, that's all! And Valentine's Day tells such a small part of the truth, covering up and leaving out all of the best that love has to offer. I think it leaves everyone in search of a little bit more.

I feel like Valentine's Day urges us to leave out love's best detail, and that detail is not a romantic comedy or a reservation—that detail is a big fat mess, full of starts and stops and second chances. Love's best details are gritty and intimate and tell the story of those who have almost lost it all, have had every reason to run away, but have kept on trying anyway.

True love is beautiful but it isn't always pretty. Valentine's Day would have us believe that true love is glossy and easily packaged. But Valentine's Day, I'm afraid, is a bit of a sham.

My husband and I are raising four kids. When the youngest was born, our oldest was only four. We often think back to our days before kids. We call them our "single days" even though we were married because it turns out children are much heavier balls and way thicker chains than a spouse. We lived in San Diego when we were "single" and did things that young and hip people do. We had a great apartment overlooking a marina. The weather was nice. We would take long walks on the beach in the evenings. We lived on an island; technically, it was a peninsula, but you get the idea. We were both working with great jobs so we had money for lots of dates. We walked to get sushi on Friday night and crepes on Sunday morning. I sat across a table starry-eyed, in a cute dress and uncomfortable shoes. We tried each other's food. We made toasts. We sang karaoke until late on the nights that we felt like feeling young, and we watched movies until late on the nights that we felt like feeling old. We slept in. *We slept in!*

And I could never say that I wasn't in love then, because I was. But, it was different. It hadn't really survived anything yet. It was a Valentine's Day kind of love.

Then, I might have been my husband's Valentine, but I wasn't his Beloved. Not yet.

* * *

I am in a beautiful Bible Study. The women it includes were Divinely jig sawed and together we make up something bigger than just ourselves. Together we make a Body. And our Body laughs too loud and talks too much and sometimes she says nothing at all. Sometimes she is full of glorious wisdom and sometimes she searches with her best intentions. Sometimes she is far too much and sometimes she is not nearly enough, but together we learn, stretch, and grow into our truest selves, whom God would have us be.

On Wednesday mornings for the last two years, we have lamented the demands of our culture. We have wrestled with the best ways to serve our God, our families, our neighbors, and ourselves all at the same time. We have complained about our motherly duties. We have been cynical about how perfectly nice people can be so irritating on Facebook. We have wondered if our kids' sports schedules should be causing this much strife. Together we have grieved insensitive husbands, lost children, demanding parents, ill siblings, competitive friends, exhausting extended family, non-believing loved ones, hateful thoughts, busy schedules, and impure hearts.

In an attempt to get down to the brass tacks of it all, simplicity, we were discussing one morning what *really* matters. What is the meaning of our life here? After all, we only have one.

Is it joy?

What brings joy?

Is it comfort?

Our culture would certainly have us think so.

But, as we complained to one another, we decided that pain-free living wasn't actually one of our goals. It might be how we are culturally trained to live, but no, comfort was not our answer. That led us to wonder if we should really just quit complaining about the ways life is uncomfortable. A long conversation ensued.

Should we be groaning this much?

Together, we came to this: Intimacy. The answer is in intimacy.

No, we would not quit complaining because groaning, well, it connects us to God. One part of the Body offered that perhaps intimacy is believing that God is big enough to deal with our situations as we are actually experiencing them, not just how we might pretend to. Another part of the Body wondered if perhaps the answer to more intimacy is having confidence in a powerful God who doesn't force us into pretending that we are just *fine*. Maybe the answer, she experimented, to truer intimacy, is believing that Christ is competent enough to deal with the problems inside our souls. He knows what our longings imply: that heaven is not here, and we are not there, and until then, nothing will be quite right! And yet another Body part shared that perhaps in the meantime, intimacy is *acknowledging* an emptiness that we simply cannot fill, will not fill, and thus our only job is to turn our longings over to Him. We agreed that intimacy is entering into pain instead of sidestepping it, acknowledging it instead of ignoring it, embracing it instead of faking it.

Together we were convinced that what God wants out of us, whom He calls Beloved, is intimacy. And intimacy is the truth. And the truth just might include some groaning. What God wants is our whole heart, not just the presentable parts, and we get one second chance after another as we try to get it right. Based on what the Body accomplished that day, we made a pact. In uniquely fingerprinted ways, we all took something with us about how to be more *intimate*. And I'm not sure it would have made the seasonal section of Target in February.

It was obvious to us all then that life is about intimacy with a loving Father, and the groaning was actually an important part of it. In a way, it was where our story *started*, paving the way for more and more honesty as God proved Himself more and more faithful to the troubled hearts of His Beloved.

My uncle and I swap music because we like poetry, mandolins, and impressing each other with our hipness. After this Bible study in particular, where we were discussing intimacy, one of the songs he sent me hit me in a tender place. There was something special about it because I thought it described well what our hearts knew that morning. It's a beautiful song on its own but at that exact moment it became Divine with its message about the man that nobody sees. As I listened, the song was describing intimacy—just what I had been talking about with brilliant women for the last hour and a half.

As I had this God-moment, I was holding my hands high to this powerful poetry. Both hands were raised at a red light and I was singing at the top of my lungs. My car often gets the truest versions of myself, both the good and the bad. It is where I am most likely to give my most honest worship and where I am most likely to cuss someone out—presumably both because no one is looking.

And there it was: the (wo)man that nobody sees. I was experiencing those very lyrics at that very moment. And it all tied in with what our Body had just accomplished. The name of the song is "When There's No One Around." Intimacy! Experiencing it all, pretty or not. Tears came as I laughed about how God can be so clever, wrapping up everything so neatly, the way only He can do. I felt like He told me that morning in three different ways that all He wants from me is *all* of me. I got it. For the first time ever, despite knowing Him for years, I finally got it.

It may sound elementary but once I figured out that life wasn't necessarily about my happiness or comfort, but was instead about intimacy, everything shifted. It was a life-changing earthquake and when the tremble of these lessons settled, nothing looked familiar. Intimacy changed the way I talked to people. I stayed and listened longer instead of rushing off or even worse, waiting to speak. It changed the way we spent money. We made fewer midday Chick-Fil-A stops and researched more about what Miss Angelina, the precious woman who helps me clean my house, might need but would never ask for. It changed our family planning. Since our home is one of our greatest gifts, we decided to open it to orphans. It changed where we lived. We moved to the middle of a banged up city so we might love our neighbor a little more easily since the poor would be right next door. After all, if intimacy was the goal, what were we doing about pursuing it? We began seeking out opportunities to connect with God, rely on Him, learn more about His character, and trust His word *enough to do what it says* rather than simply paint ourselves a pretty story.

Intimacy, we are discovering, is in the details. It is in acknowledging what makes us uncomfortable and inviting God there, listening for His voice, examining His teachings, and doing what He would have us do. Intimacy is in not leaving anything out, hoarding our favorite parts of our story and keeping them all to ourselves, or denying the truth and insisting that God mind His own business. Intimacy is approaching every endeavor with the question, "How might I find you here, Lord?"

Before I sought to adopt intimacy as a way of life, I would have stopped at the Peninsula-Marina-Overlooking-Apartment-Sushi-Dates-and-Beach-Strolls story about my husband. I would've stopped at Valentine's Day. Because the real story would never make it into the seasonal section at Target.

* * *

My husband is the best thing that has ever happened to me. I say that unequivocally and mean it. He is my most tangible proof that God is wild about me. However, our first year of marriage was a little rocky. We had moved from Japan and were living in San Diego, which, with its beaches, zillion dollar homes, and perfect weather, frankly felt nothing like home, my piece of Texas that I loved. I just felt far away from anything familiar and the one person whom I had to rely on was really kind of ticking me off.

While we didn't get married *that* late in life, it was later than most of our friends and was enough time to accumulate plenty of baggage and develop a lot of bad habits. We were also both quite used to calling our own shots and had a lot to learn about teamwork. We had gotten away with a lot in the years leading up to one another. Intensely in love, but broken, prideful, selfish, and immature, we were bad at marriage. We were missing each other, like parallel train tracks, never quite crossing paths. And we were fighting a lot. It was a lonely time for me. Not one single thing in our marriage was coming easily.

Our apartment was next to a couple's who only visited twice a year, meaning it was primarily empty. I remember being so thankful that we did not share walls with anyone. Our marriage did not need a witness.

After an awful fight the night before, one day I texted my husband letting him know that I would not be coming home after work (something he would never do). I didn't know where I was going, but it wouldn't be anywhere near him. In Valentine's Day cards, even the fights are romantic. Has anyone else noticed that? *You forgot to take the trash out?! Again?! Oh, you!* But there is nothing romantic about crying in an empty library and googling if proper etiquette says you should return wedding gifts if you only stayed married eight months.

I taught middle school at the time, so after school let out, I went home and packed a bag of essentials, and went downtown to just walk around because I didn't have a plan yet and needed fresh air. I walked around with a knot the size of my fist where my heart should have been and tried not to draw attention to myself. I cried looking for a hotel that didn't cost too much but wasn't scary.

Downtown there were always people asking for money, holding up their signs. And this time, as I walked those streets avoiding my life, for the first time ever, I felt a kinship with those people and their signs. The signs that touched me the most were the ones that said "Need help." I needed help. And I felt pretty homeless. So I did something I had never done before. I sat down next to someone who was asking for money. Her sign said, "We all need grace—anything helps." The word "grace" caught my attention. I had never seen that one before. I assumed she was a believer. And she had on Wrangler jeans, too much eyeliner, and had teased her hair, it seemed. All of these things reminded me of home, so I liked her right away. I happened to have a pocket full of quarters because I would sometimes bribe my unruly students with them, and she had a little dog with her, so it was easy to sit down and make conversation. The dog provided a risk-free audience and my pocket full of change was insurance that I had at least a little something to offer.

With my hand out for her dog to sniff, I knelt down beside her and eventually put my back up on the same wall she was leaning against. When she saw I was getting comfortable, she looked at me and said, "Hey honey." I smiled, probably a bit wearily, and asked her how she was doing. She said, "I'm hanging in there. How are you, honey?" And for some reason—maybe it was her jeans, maybe it was that she called me honey, probably it was her dog—I told her the truth. I can't explain why it felt right to share the intimate details of my life, but I told her that I wasn't sure my marriage was gonna make it. I told her I didn't understand how two people could love each other so fiercely and yet hurt each other so deeply. I told her that I was lonely and that I wanted to go home. I told her that my mom's house smelled like roast and that was where I really wanted to be. I told her I wanted to start over. A redo. I needed a redo.

She let me talk for a while. She stared at her shoes. She didn't say a word. But when she looked up her eyes were filled with tears and they told me that she understood exactly how I felt. Her eyes told me that everything I had just said was part of her story too. And she hugged me.

It was kind of awkward after that because I didn't know what to say anymore and it seemed she had committed to not saying anything. Maybe somewhere along her journey she had learned that was best. So I reached in my pocket and gave her a handful of quarters. She took them and patted me on the knee. I talked to her dog a little bit and then said I should probably get going. As I stood up, she asked me my name. When I told her, she said she would pray for me. The person asking for change was going to pray for me. My eyes welled up and I asked her her name. Ruth. Her name was Ruth. I told her I would pray for her too. As I walked away she said, "The answer is in grace, honey.

Second chance is just a name. You can't ever run out of second chances, honey. You're not the only one who needs a redo. We all do. That husband of yours, too."

Something completely supernatural happened immediately after I shared that wall with Ruth. I stood up, turned around, and walked the exact path that I had just walked except this time facing the other direction. A completely different view was in front of me, seeing the exact same objects from the other side. There is no doubt that my different perspective was Divine because, trust me, I have some very impressive biceps for carrying grudges. But all of a sudden I wasn't angry. Not only was I willing to go home and forgive my husband and ask for his forgiveness too, but I was actually excited to. I raced to our tiny apartment to try to make it as homey as possible in there before he got home. I tidied up. I lit candles. I put on our favorite music. I made a roast.

Even though there was no way to explain my heart, I prepared what I would say when my husband walked through the door. I would just tell him that while I was vacuuming I heard Dr. Phil say that every relationship needed a hero and that I really wanted to be our hero. I didn't know how to do that but I promised to keep trying to learn. And then I would tell him that I made a new friend named Ruth and she told me something about how second chances weren't really second chances and I think that second chances just might be where our story *starts*. And I'm ready to start. Again. Because we all need grace.

From the window, I watched him walk up our stairs expecting me not to be there. He was holding flowers upside down, with the blooms all wrong. Were they just in case? He opened the door to our home that smelled like love and me standing there sheepish. He was thrilled to see me and couldn't hide it. He dropped the flowers on their heads and scooped me up. Even though we were in this awful fight and no reconciliation had happened there was something about seeing each other in that moment that made us forget it all. We grinned knowing that there was a lot of work to do but also knowing that together we would do it, whatever it was. Our grins turned into nervous laughter as we hugged with a junior high type of vulnerability. And to this day, he still doesn't know about Ruth. I never had a chance to tell him.

* * *

I think about what our Body taught itself that day of Bible study and know that it's true. Intimacy is in acknowledging, embracing, and celebrating the ways that we struggle. It's those second chances that have turned my husband and me into each other's Beloved. They are where our story has started and thickened and triumphed and become breathtakingly beautiful. Our story is ours. Only ours. It is something that no one else would ever want. Unique, fitting, intimate. Starts and stops and second chances. Beloved.

God craves our intimacy. The Lord reveals this desire of His in a way that tickles me. Throughout scripture, He asks questions He already knows the answer to. He does it often and I think it's possible that He is trying to see just how intimate we are willing to be. How much are we willing to give Him? Just the "good" stuff? Or all of it? Are we going to spill it? Or not? Are we willing to return home? And if so, carrying what of our time away?

God asks Adam, in the garden, *Where are you? Who told you you were naked? Have you eaten from the tree, Adam?* (Genesis 3:9-11) He of course knew the answers to all of these questions, but was Adam willing to admit his failure? Was Adam willing to have a real relationship?

Then there is this one from Jesus from the shore: *So, boys, did you catch any fish?* (John 21:5). He knew they hadn't had any luck at all that night. But what would they say? Would they let Him in? Or would a pat answer, "Not many," give the intended, "Why don't you mind your own business?"

Or this one, at the well, also from Jesus: *So, daughter, why don't you go get your husband?* (John 4:16). He knew that she had five. But what would she say? Would she let Him love her anyway? Despite her mess?

Do we want a second chance or not?

God knows it's where our story starts, turning us into more than just a pretty package, prideful and plastic. Intimacy turns us into His Beloved.

In Luke 15, Jesus tells us a parable about a man who had two sons. The younger son did the unthinkable and asked for his inheritance early. He might as well have said, "I wish you were dead." Amazingly, the father obliges this outrageous request and divides his wealth. "And not many days later, the younger son gathered everything together and went on a journey into a distant country, and there he squandered his estate with loose living." (Luke 15:13) It didn't take long for the young son's plans to fall apart. There was a famine. He was broke. Desperate for work, he worked in the fields with pigs, unclean animals. He was so destitute and uncared for that he longed for what the pigs were eating. "And he would have gladly filled his stomach with the pods that the swine were eating, and no one was giving anything to him." (Luke 15:16)

Eventually the young son came to his senses and realized that it was in his father's home that he had plenty, more than enough. So he planned to return home and prepared a speech to ask for a place as a hired servant, surely all that he deserved. "But **while he was still a long way off**, his father saw him and felt compassion for him, and ran and embraced him and kissed him." **(emphasis mine)** (Luke 15:20) The son started to give his speech but the father didn't even let him finish before ordering the servants to dress him in the best robe, place a ring on his finger, sandals on his feet, and prepare for him the fattest calf and most joyful of celebrations.

But. When the older son heard the celebration, he became very angry. He refused to join the party. The father pleaded with him to see it his way, but the older son yelled that he had done everything exactly right and had never been given a thing. The father assured him that he had always been with him and everything he had was his also, but now was a time for celebration.

The prodigal son tells love's intimate story so completely. Jesus' longest parable doesn't leave anything out. I love this parable for the same reasons that everyone else does. It is so rich. A selfish yet repentant young man, a petulant and prideful older brother, a merciful and loving father—I have been all of these characters: quick to squander, slow to celebrate, yearning to be forgiven, reluctant to hand it out, longing, pining, waiting for love to return and racing to meet it when it does. From every angle, this story grabs me.

I have taken too much of what wasn't ever mine and lived in excess just to realize that I had it all wrong. I have worn my righteousness on my sleeve but not in my heart. I have focused on how the love in my life was packaged, concentrating only on presentation, and rejected the beauty of struggle. I have insisted that one shouldn't need a second chance, and that pretending to have it all right was actually the more beautiful way. I have returned home with lengthy speeches prepared, just to be scooped up by a lover who didn't care to hear.

The pure of heart rejoice at the telling of this story. We root for the success of the underdog knowing that his success is ours also. His failures actually boast the beauty of his return. God's running reception, encouraging us to trust Him fully, pursue Him more. But this time, pursue Him with great, great thanks in a story well-told for not leaving anything out, however battered, however bruised it may be.

The prodigal son so completely tells all of love's story. And it would never make the seasonal section at Target. A young son given into prostitutes and returning home covered in the stench of an unclean animal is a little too gritty, no? A pouting older brother resentful of all that God is willing to hand out to those who are undeserving yelling, "MINE MINE MINE!" like a preschooler is a little too undistinguished, don't you think? A hopeful and waiting father willing to pull up his robe and sprint after his Beloved still a long way off and cover him in kisses is a little too unsettling, isn't it?

But Jesus' longest parable tells the *whole* story regardless of how our polished culture feels about the details.

Covering something up is the same thing as lying and it has the same effect on our spirit. And I've heard there are three things that won't be put off long—the sun, the moon, and the truth.

Beloved love is not always romantic but it is always real—a sprinting, covered in pig stench, drop those flowers on their heads kind of love. And God craves real love. God is not content with Valentine's Day love. And truthfully, I think a lot of times we are. When it comes to God, we are fine with a love pretty enough to package. We are fine with a love that hasn't been tested and tried. In a contest, Beloved Love kicks the butt of Valentine's Day Love every single time. Valentine's Day can't even get lucky because Beloved Love has muscles that are actually used, not just flexed.

The prodigal son realized that His father had better ideas about how to nourish him, and he didn't have to run away from home in order to groan. He could groan right where he was and know that His father had compassion for him. Sharing the struggle might actually have been a faith builder as his father fattened calves and smothered him in kisses when he walked his path aware that his father's ways were better than his own. If the prodigal son would have just shared his troubles with a willingness to be intimate, would he have ever had to leave? If he would have trusted his father to be able to handle his complicated emotions, would there have been anything to confess? Whatever the case, this story is made beautiful for the finding out. Let us all give up foolish desires that leave us dirty and hungry and far from home. Let us trust that intimacy is more important, whatever it promises, and return home to the waiting One who knows that we all need another second chance. Again.

"So, as those who have been chosen of God, holy and beloved, put on a heart of compassion, kindness, humility, gentleness and patience." (Colossians 3:12)

To Consider:

1. Do you tend to embrace your heartaches or gloss over them? Would you consider yourself more dramatic than stoic or vice versa? How does this affect your relationships/your relationship with God?

2. Do you believe that the Lord can handle your complexities? Does your faith life prove it?

3. In what ways are you comfortable letting intimacy rule your life? In what ways are you uncomfortable?

4. How do you relate to each character of the Prodigal Son? Is there one character that is easier or more difficult to relate to? Be specific.

To Practice:

For one week consider praying and meditating on the prayer "Whatever it takes, Lord, increase my intimacy with you."

To Listen:

1. "Lord I'm Ready Now" by Plumb
2. "My Beloved" by Kari Jobe

PAPER

Covering gift of

love, never-ending. Hiding

flaws. Holy like You.

CHAPTER 4:

Baal, Bargaining, & Life Saving Grace

"Are we in love with God or just His stuff?"
— FRANCIS CHAN

Much of my ministry with young women involves public speaking. This is unfortunate for me. I have a love/hate relationship with speaking to large groups— heavy on hate and light on love.

Initially it sounds like a great idea. I am always so flattered to be asked in the first place so I start daydreaming about topics and trying to think of funny jokes. In my mind, I'm so winsome, making the crowd laugh and cry in all the right places. I conjure up the applause that comes afterwards and then practice sheepish smiles in the mirror. I immediately start thinking of which shoes I should wear.

But then, the reality of actually speaking... out loud... while other people listen... sets in and I start to obsess about writer's block and stage fright. Even if a good message does come to mind to share, I convince myself that once I get up there I'm going to forget it all and end up just standing there smiling in a pair of really cute shoes. The stress leads to fever blisters and breakouts. And then, finally, tears.

I obsess about a perfect message containing just the right balance of light and heavy, eat my nails to the quick, and become cantankerous and difficult to live with. My husband slinks around half-afraid of me and reminds me that speaking my heart really shouldn't be so difficult on my skin or our marriage. I catch him tiptoeing around me trying not to make a mess and realize that I've finally done it. I've become so unbearable that my husband is going to leave me for Kim Kardashian. I warn him that Kanye is no one to be trifled with and assure him that KK would have none of what is under our kitchen sink. He then pats me on the head and goes for a run. The long route.

I get more comfortable as each year goes by but even still, when it comes time to prepare for our college retreat season, I am heavy laden with the pressure of responsibility. I long to carry out the assignment well. I understand that God wants me needy, so I'm sure it's no coincidence that the words don't always come effortlessly when it is time to write and that nerves are a big part of my preparing process.

I spend a lot of time praying and begging while staring at a blank computer screen. I hope that something worth listening to will come to mind for God and me to write together. I beg shamelessly for God just to please show up. As I grovel, that little cursor thingy on my computer just blinks away. It taunts me with its consistency. It's quite badgering, really. So I beg God some more. I have resorted to some ridiculous things while trying to get His attention.

I promise to give Him a standing ovation once He whispers some words in my ear.

I go back and fix all my typos thinking He will be more likely to show up if the page is tidier.

I promise never to gossip or yell at my kids ever again if I could just have one brilliant idea.

And then, lastly, I compromise. God, it doesn't have to be brilliant anymore. Just give me anything. Leftovers are fine.

And I know how silly this sounds. Trust me, I do.

As I was going through all this hoopla preparing for our latest retreat, I happened to be reading in 1 Kings. The Word is living indeed, because God directed me to Elijah at exactly the right time.

Elijah was one of God's great prophets. And one day he found himself in a not so friendly competition with 450 other prophets of the pagan god, Baal. They were fighting over who served the one true God and they had come up with a contest to settle the score.

The rules of the contest were simple: whomever's god showed up and set fire to a prepared sacrifice was the servant of the one true God. Who was going to show up with fire? God or Baal?

The prophets of Baal spent all day trying to get their god's attention. They yelled out, sang, danced, and even cut themselves in order to add their own blood to the sacrifice. It was all very dramatic. Elijah, entertained, just watched. In my mind, he was leaning on a tree with his hands in his pockets or maybe he was calmly inspecting his fingernails, but either way he had a smirk on his face, smugly watching the show.

When Baal didn't show up despite all the theatrics, Elijah suggested that perhaps Baal was just sleeping. Or, no, perhaps Baal was deep in thought. Or, I know! Perhaps Baal was traveling. Yes, that's it! Elijah suggested that the prophets probably just needed to yell louder. This Elijah was a smart aleck, was he not? So the prophets danced, pleaded, yelled, and added more blood to the sacrifice.

Nothing happened.

After the loud, messy chaos and a fair bit of taunting from Elijah, it was his turn to call on God.

And Elijah may have been a smart aleck, but when he had faith, he had F-A-I-T-H, an all-caps kind of FAITH. For Elijah knew his Lord.

So he showed off.

Not only did he ask God to come down to the altar with fire, but he asked God to come down to the wet altar with fire. Elijah asked that the altar be soaked with water three times.

And then, he prayed.

The result was immediate.

Fire came down and burned up the soaking wet altar. The hundreds of people watching this death match fell flat on their faces and shouted out to the one true God, Elijah's God.

What I took away from this, as I was preparing for our retreat, was that I was acting a little like a prophet of Baal with all the dramatics. I begged God to please come through for me, making promises and demands, and altogether screaming out with a lot of hoopla, just short of shedding my own blood.

But with Elijah, there was no hoopla.

And God didn't demand it. There was no yelling, no dancing, no blood spilled.

Essentially, what it came down to was God's love and Elijah's faith in that love.

I realized I had a lot to learn. I had a humbling realization that perhaps I wasn't truly certain of God's love for me, not like Elijah was anyway.

No matter how mature in my faith I am, I realize that I just can't quit asking that question. How do you feel about me? Do you love me?

Aren't we always trying to figure it out? I don't know about you, but for me, it has the potential to go like this:

God, if you're there and you love me—You'll fix this situation for me.

And then, to ensure that He comes through for me when I need Him to, I do something that I think will impress Him, like, say, attend a retreat or read more.

A lot like Baal's prophets, I find myself bargaining with God. *God, if you help me write this speech, I will go through the gospels and wake up earlier for quiet times.*

But, Elijah! He just asked in faith and waited for God to show up knowing that no matter what, he would be victorious.

I have spent much of my life bargaining with God.

But do you know what?

Now that I think about it, really think about it, bargaining wasn't about getting what I wanted out of God. Because the truth is that I was fine without the fixed situation or with standing in front of a crowd staring at my cute shoes with nothing to say.

The bargaining wasn't about my desires, not really. The bargaining was about my desire to know that *He cared*. What I wanted was proof that He would show up if I asked Him to, because that would mean He was willing to involve Himself in my daily life in ways that mattered to me. Bargaining was an attempt to know that He really loved me! Answering my demands would prove that He loved me in a way that I understood as love.

I had a realization that bargaining was my attempt to find out whom I was dealing with. The question was really, *how much do you love me?*

Do you love me enough to care about my life? Enough to worry about my worries? Enough to give me the desires of my heart? *Do you care about my heart?*

Bargaining is just how I thought I would finally be able to see and touch His devotion. I thought that answered prayers and blessings were the best way to see His devotion. I crave God's attention. I long for God's participation in my daily life. I long to know that He loves me, and I have gone about some really goofy ways to try to prove that it is so.

But there is a better way.

God has already proved exactly whom we are dealing with. He has shown us with so much passion exactly how much He cares about us. It is thick and dynamic and beautiful and against the grain and relieving and controversial.

But our way of life—with ourselves as the center of our story and our insistence on living as comfortably as possible—it is a barrier to seeing the actual way that God has told us that He loves us.

Consumed by the things around us instead of the eternal things above us, we can't rightly see how great His love is.

God is not preoccupied with our comfort, even if *we* are. If comfort is our love language, His love language is a little more... intense, a little grittier. He is not sending us valuable trinkets, effortless relationships, instant remedies, magic wands, or gift cards from Target.

He sent us HIMSELF instead.

Our pain-free living with all of our desires neatly around us and in place is not proof of His love for us!

Jesus is.

God came down. He walked down to our level. He walked this Earth and shook it up and turned it upside down and inside out. He got His hands dirty and His heart broken. He left heaven, where peace reigned, to enter a messy, fallen, broken world where He was spat upon and mocked and misunderstood and murdered and left all alone. He loved with such controversial, counterintuitive love that people literally could not understand it. It was so selfless, so great, so easy that they rejected it. God left the glories of Heaven to become nothing. Nothing.

Why?

Because He wants to stroll with us in the cool of the evening. He wants to walk beside us and point out the beauties that He has made for us. Because He loves us.

He completely set aside His glory to really speak to you and me, for us to know how much He meant it. Because He wasn't just going to do this, but He was going to do this dramatically. It was going to hurt. It was going to cost Him because maybe then we would *know*. Maybe then we would understand. If He gave it all away, maybe then we would really believe how important we are to Him. He wants to be with us. See? He gave it all away. For us.

God is more loving than we have ever imagined Him to be. Even when those *things* aren't falling into our laps like we have hoped.

So how do we know?

Because He gave us His very self.

He has already decided to answer us. Before we ever asked.

* * *

In Matthew 12:38-42, Jesus had some harsh words for the Pharisees and teachers of the Law who were demanding a miraculous sign from Him. He said that asking for a sign was wicked and adulterous and assured them they would never receive what they were after. He brought up the prophet Jonah and said, "for just as Jonah was three days and three nights in the belly of the sea monster, so will the Son of Man be three days and three nights in the heart of the earth." (Matthew 12:40) Jesus let them know that Someone far greater than Jonah had come. In short, a grand miracle had already taken place.

The Pharisees had very specific ideas about how God would look and what He would do once He was here. Because of the oppression they and their ancestors had experienced and because of their current condition —under strict rule of the Romans—they were very enthusiastic about a Savior to finally come and deliver them. The problem was that, well... when God came, He wasn't exactly what they were expecting.

They were expecting a powerful political force and just knew that the promised Savior would be someone who would empower them, someone who would be impossible to defeat. They were certain that this Savior would care about the things they cared about and consequently grant them their desires, the pain-free living that they had in mind. These people longed for freedom and were sure that a Savior would deliver it. For all their hard work and careful living, they were anxious to collect on the blessings owed them. After all, they were a righteous people.

But that's not what they got.

And so they largely dismissed Him and His message.

Jesus was hard for this Jewish culture to recognize. He was a carpenter from Nazareth. That's like saying God was a mechanic from Snook, Texas. If you don't know much about Snook, you don't have to. It's practically onomatopoeia. But Snook and His village are almost the exact same size. Can you imagine? *I'm a mechanic from Snook. Follow me.*

He was hardly a political heavyweight. He didn't seem to care at all about having important friends or playing political games with those in power. Jews might have gone to hear him speak, expecting a rallying speech about how *the Jewish people won't be held down, not any longer! Now is the time to revolt, to break free, to rise again!* But when they got there, ready to take notes about militant strategies, instead they heard about how the meek were the ones who were blessed, about how the kingdom belonged to the poor in spirit.

What?

Jesus' way might have been more confounding than relieving. *What kind of God are you?! Can we just get back to driving out Rome, and my pain-free living, because I think that's how I will recognize you better?*

But what was happening all around them that they were refusing to see was GRACE. Their own expectations of the Messiah blinded them to the truth.

It's so easy to be frustrated with the Pharisees and consider them fools for their tunnel vision, but it seems paradoxical to claim to have nothing in common with them. It seems pretty Pharisee-like not to be able to relate to the Pharisees. Because don't we also harbor our own personal expectations of life, blinding us to the Lord's wonderful plan? Don't we also insist on miracles because we have forgotten or grown bored with the most important one?

As Jesus scolded the Pharisees for their blindness, He was also revealing how humankind would be redeemed. Just as the prophet Jonah was swallowed by a big fish, spending three days and three nights in its belly, Jesus would also spend three days and three nights in the grave. And just as Jonah came out of the fish restoring the Ninevites, so Jesus would rise from the grave drawing humanity to the Truth.

We are not unlike the Pharisees insisting that God abide by the systems we have created, that He love us the way we deem important, that He deliver us from our trials. In Matthew 12, Jesus points us to Jonah, who overcame death and redeemed the Ninevites, much like He, through His resurrection, overcomes death and reunites us with God. He is our proof that God is mighty and faithful to His promises. *He* is our miracle.

* * *

I simply can't get enough of Johnnie Moore's book, *Dirty God: Jesus in the Trenches*. Despite ingesting his words like essential nutrients the first time I read it, I now keep it on my bedside table and leaf through it regularly. I want to be reminded of the sustenance it gave during a bankrupt time where my faith was frail. In it, Moore talks about a near-death experience he had and how there was something about the experience that was actually sweet. I was reminded of my own near-death experience and recalled the new life it brought.

I was seven or eight years old. I lived next to a golf course. My girlfriend and I loved to play on the golf course right at dusk when the golfers were finishing up. We would play in the sand pits, do gymnastics on the long soft green grass, antagonize the geese, and feed the ducks. We probably did this at least three times a week. We knew what time to go so no one would get mad at us. We knew which sand pits had the cat poop, which houses to avoid because the husband was grumpy, how far to push each goose before being attacked, and what kind of bread the ducks liked the best. We were experts at playing on the golf course after hours.

To get there we had to cut through people's backyards. The backyard most convenient for us to use happened to have a big German Shepherd in it, but he lived on a leash. We never quite befriended him. In fact he would bark at us wildly as we ran through his yard, but we were always gone in a flash, his bark extra motivation to get to where we were going. While we respected his presence and didn't tease or taunt him (he was huge!), we certainly didn't worry about him either. He was tied up.

One night after hearing my dad's whistle for us to come home, we took off on our familiar path. We ran across the yard we always ran through. The dog barked as he always did. But this time it was a different bark. I can't explain it, but I knew right away with the sound of the first bark, that he was saying something different. If every other time we ran through his yard his bark said, *I wish I could chase you*, this bark said, *I am going to chase you, I am going to catch you, and I am going to eat you*. Alarmed, I turned around. Sure enough, Mr. German Shepherd was not tied up. And not only was he not tied up, but he was in a full four-legged snarling German Shepherd sprint.

My first instinct was to turn around and just keep running as fast as I could, but I only took half a step before knowing with everything in me that was a mistake. I knew this dog could outrun me and was about to in milliseconds.

Without thinking, another instinct took over. I very much had an out of body experience. I can't explain it, but without knowing what was coming next and seemingly in slow motion, I stopped running, I turned around and looked at that dog. I stood squarely, and I yelled with a voice I didn't know that I had and from somewhere down very deep,

"SIT!"

If I'm lying, I'm dying, the dog sat. My friend was long gone and I inched away while staring hard at the dog trying to communicate the words, *don't mess with me, you don't want none.*

I eventually caught up with my friend. We lay on the grass together panting, in shock and awe, trying to fully absorb what had just happened, the miracle that we had just been a part of, the way that we had been delivered, the very unexpected way that we had been saved. We just couldn't get our minds around it. We couldn't say much except, *I can't believe that just happened.* We appreciated the magnitude.

It was a miracle. We saw it as such. I was only seven or eight at the time and I certainly wasn't articulate enough to describe it then, but I went home feeling different. In those few short seconds, I saw my life flash before me. But those seconds seemed to mature me. My knees were shaky but my appreciation was sure. The air was a little lighter, easier to breathe. My fluttering heart seemed to dance around in my chest with great, great thanks. This miracle took me somewhere different. My vision was clearer and in better focus. The things that I was angry about seemed, all of a sudden, quite silly. I can't tell you how long it lasted, but for a good while, my perspective just seemed to mature into knowing what mattered and what really didn't. I interacted with my friends differently. I appreciated my parents in new ways. Everything seemed to slow down a bit. Now like I said, I don't know how long this lasted, but I am certain, considering those revelations and my gratefulness for them, that experience is one I would have done well to meditate on often.

The sad truth is that my friend and I grew quite used to the story and it became just that: a story. That miracle changed from a death-defying tale of the most unlikely, life-changing drama that made us reverent and thankful to just breathe air, into something that we shared around the lunch table. It became a story to entertain our friends, making them guess what came next, with ourselves being the stars of every scene.

We grew used to our miracle. We made the miracle about us instead of Him who performed it. We looked for what our miracle might gain us instead of continuing to live in great, great thanks of it.

The greatest miracle was about a second chance. It was about GRACE. We have just forgotten or grown used to it. We need not demand more. For there is none greater.

Forgetting the miracle leads us to believe that we have room to ask how to be loved by God. We think we know how He can love us best. And it's ludicrous because we are already being loved. It has already happened.

We can quit bargaining with God. There's no need to shout to wake Him up. We already have God's attention.

As we come to more fully appreciate what God has done for us, let us remember the miraculous gift that was given by God. Let us not forget that the Messiah came and took upon Himself the penalty that we deserve for our sin so that those who place their faith in Him would have everlasting life.

Let us finally start appreciating amazing grace.

*"And He has said to me, '**My grace is sufficient for you**, for power is perfected in weakness.' Most gladly, therefore, I will rather boast about my weaknesses, so that the power of Christ may dwell in me...."* **(emphasis mine)** *(2 Corinthians 12:9)*

TO CONSIDER:

1. Have you ever found yourself bargaining with God? About what? What does what you bargain over say about what you hold dear?

2. Do you believe that God's affection equals your happy life? Do you believe that your blessings equal God's pleasure? Do you believe that darkness equals His displeasure?

3. How does your love language differ from God's?

4. How do you try to work God into your system? In what ways do you tell Him what is important instead of searching out what He thinks is important?

TO PRACTICE:

Journal about a time that death felt near. Conjure up your exact emotions.

TO LISTEN:

1. "Good Good Father" by Housefires

2. "From the Day" by I am They

CHAPTER 5:

Jesus & the Crazies

*"Our hearts of stone become hearts of flesh when
we learn where the outcast weeps."*
—BRENNAN MANNING

About five years ago, my husband and I moved to a new town—finally, after years of bouncing around—to start our real, grownup, not-moving-anywhere-ever-again life. Even though we were ready to move and we knew our last home was a temporary one, it grieved us deeply to leave it.

There would be much to miss about Minnesota.

In so many ways it was there that we learned how to be grownups. That freezing little town enveloped and nurtured us in our young marriage. Being married took on new meaning as we navigated those first years of what it truly meant to become one on a deeper level than just playing house. We learned that love was something tried and true, not something glittery and gold.

We brought two babies home to the first home we ever owned. We watched them learn to smile and laugh and walk and talk between those walls. I'll never forget the layout of the house, those rooms and halls where my babies played their first games.

We had wonderful neighbors who came over for parties and tolerated our rascally dogs who did not understand property lines when it came to going number two. They took care of us as my husband worked crazy hours finishing his medical training. They would bring over dinner and shovel our drive.

Minnesota was a great start, and to this day, I viscerally miss the way the air smells in fall and the way the sky looks before a snow storm.

But, of all that there was to grieve about, the biggest loss would be no longer living minutes away from the girlfriends that I made while living there. The best way to describe what I had with that circle of women was *True*. It was not always pretty, but it was always *True*. I celebrated my place in that circle.

There is really nothing romantic about it; we were just a bunch of moms living life together. But we did it well. We shared each other's special moments and endured each other's mundane. We walked into each other's kitchens and put away the dishes in the sink without having to ask where anything went, and then went to the fridge and asked why we were out of flavored creamer. We fought, we cried, we laughed until we couldn't breathe. We resented and then forgave, and then resented and then forgave again, each other's siblings, parents, and husbands. We disciplined each other's children and did each other's laundry—boxer shorts and all. We ran each other's errands and fed each other when the going got tough. Our kids wore each other's clothes, caught each other's colds, and will probably make out with each other one day, although we can't be certain because we're not there yet. We shared prayer requests, joys and frustrations, the highs and the lows, and that precious moment in time. And I wept an ugly weep, pulling away in the moving van. They were why.

I don't know if it was my unrealistic expectations, the stage of life we were in, or the high bar my girlfriends set, but making friends once we moved wasn't happening with timely ease. I expected to fall into new friendships as if friendship was this one big thing instead of a million tiny things. I sulked. And I felt lonely. And I missed my life.

A couple of weeks into my sulking, I was asked by an acquaintance from my college days, someone well plugged into this new community of mine, to talk to a group of student chaplains about how they could more effectively minister to the wilder girls in their organizations. These wilder girls were affectionately dubbed by the student chaplains, their peers, as "the crazies," and the meeting that I was to speak at was called "How to Reach the Crazies."

I was thrilled. First of all, I was thrilled to be asked to be a part of something. I was missing my pack and my community, and I felt enthusiastic about the inclusion. And secondly, while any invitation might have consoled me, this invitation felt like a special one because this acquaintance seemed to understand me as being someone who struggles with a bit of an identity crisis—a little bit chaplain, a little bit "crazy."

You see, I have always wanted to be crazier than I am, more daring. I have an alter ego and she is covered in tattoos. I love her because she's just a *little* bit crazy. My alter ego doesn't have the filter that I do. She always goes with her first impulse regardless of how radical. She never writes things on a calendar. Her hair is some radiant, unnatural color. She shoots from the hip. She isn't deterred by much. And like I said, she has way more tattoos.

But, honestly, I have had to face it, I am a soccer mom. Thus, the identity crisis. I drive a very practical suburban vehicle. I do my laundry on a certain day of the week. I cut crusts off of sandwiches. I consider my highlights sassy. And I am way more likely to pick up two new pacifiers (where *do* they go?!) rather than two new tattoos.

I have an identity crisis, and it appeared that my old acquaintance and possibly new friend understood it. I was thrilled. She saw me as someone who could relate to the "crazies," but was really a chaplain at heart. Or, maybe she saw me as someone who could relate to the chaplains, but was really a "crazy" at heart? Yes! I hoped for the latter one and started preparing my talk.

My bullet points were along these lines: (1) If we don't have true love for the "crazies" then our words are a clanging cymbal. (2) It is humility, not piety that is going to show them Christ. (3) Our love works like a magnet. And then I threw in at the last minute that (4) a little humor didn't hurt anyone.

That was all well and good.

Fine.

It was a nice night.

But I went home unsettled. After some tossing and turning and prayer, this question plagued me: *How in the Sam Hill do you talk about winning people to Christ only barely talking about who Christ is?!* I thought about how those "crazies" sure would love Jesus if they really knew who He was, and I wished my message to the chaplains would have been that simple.

"Girls!" I should have said, "Tell them, the 'crazies,' who Jesus really is! Not who our Christian subculture has created Him to be, but who He really is! Not some pharisaical version of Him, but the true version! The version that rooted for sinners! They'll love it. I know they will."

"Tell them that Jesus loved the outcast. And girls, do you want to know who the outcast was? And is?! Well, I just sat around a table with you where we spent two hours calling a group of people 'the crazies,' so I have a hint—**it's not us**! We aren't the outcasts, the 'crazies' are! And Jesus' heart bleeds for them. That's right. And the outcasts' hearts? Well, they were completely transformed by the acceptance they received from Him. Hear that? The acceptance. Never the shame. So, maybe we should rethink all these labels we give people. Maybe we should understand them as people who sin differently than us and call them 'sister' instead. Maybe 'sister,' not 'crazy,' is what is more humble... Christ-like... *True*."

"And before these precious people who sin differently than you tune you out, you should promise them something. Promise them not to use churchy words that make you feel holy and them feel shameful. No fancy words. You should probably also promise not to say confusing things like 'God told me' or 'I heard Him say' or 'He came to me' or 'It's been put on my heart' or a million other Christian subculture colloquialisms that make people outside of that subculture roll their eyes. Let's try not to give them a reason to roll their eyes just yet. Let's stick to the facts and avoid the confusing stuff for a while."

"And, after you get that out of the way, girls, we need to tell them about Jesus! All about Him! Don't you know they will just love Him?! I think you should tell them (I think they'd be glad to hear) that Jesus would rather be at their party than ours. He would! His friends, when He was here, were more like them than us. It's true! And He took hits for it. They should know that. People called Him a drunkard and a glutton because of the company He kept. But He loved them deeply and He served them to the end."

"In fact, what did He say about those other people who claimed that He shouldn't be hanging out with such a crowd? He called them snakes, vipers, actors, and white-washed tombs, meaning they looked pretty on the outside but on the inside were simply full of dead things. He took up for those crazies and He didn't care what it cost Him.

When it came time for Jesus to choose His inner circle to help Him change the world, divide a calendar, and bring Good News, He chose a motley crew. He chose everyday folks, not the ones who excelled at religious school like He was supposed to. He chose the passed over instead of the elite. Isn't that just great?! Jesus chose the passed over to help Him bring God to this world."

"Then, if you still have their attention, you could tell them about how rebellious Jesus was. Jesus turned things upside down in a way I just know they would appreciate. You could explain how He broke all of society's silly rules and ticked people off doing it. Jesus talked to people He wasn't supposed to talk to. He touched people He wasn't supposed to touch. He ate with people He wasn't supposed to eat with. He went to people's houses He should have been repulsed by. He worked when He wasn't supposed to work. He was labeled a troublemaker. He caused a stir and He didn't back off. Don't you think that they will just love that? He was a rebel! Kind of like them. He wasn't bound by a bunch of rules! Kind of like them. He was really annoyed by the people that kept the rules perfectly and thought themselves better than everyone else because of it! Kind of like them. And perhaps they know Him better than we think they do and just don't realize yet. I think I'm starting to understand. I think I'm finally learning."

"Girls, when you think of Jesus, I want you to consider these things. He chose them, too. It's their house He wants to visit. It's them that He called down from the tree. They are whom He met at the well. They are whom He reached out to touch. For them He drew in the sand. Around His table He wants the partiers, the selfish, the lonely, the mentally ill, the cheaters, the oppressed, and the judged. He wants the promiscuous, the homeless, the sick, the movie stars, the ones on Wall

Street, the addicts, the ones caught up in bad choice after bad choice, and the ones with broken hearts. They are deeply, deeply loved. As are you. Where around the table do you fit, sister? You see that you are called there too, don't you? Our job, as someone sitting at that table, is to tell of the love of Christ. Not to anyone especially, but to all of us equally. For we are all equally in need."

"I'm sorry that I have never put it this plainly before. My prayer for us is that we recognize this gift of Jesus' invitation. I pray that we receive it like a child and just keep showing up to the table He so eagerly invited us to. I pray that we know that we are accepted, all of us, by Something so much bigger than us."

"So, I think we should ask if we could just start over, if they'll let us, because I know we have some Good News. Let's just start there."

I thought about what I wished I had said, and I wondered why it wasn't more obvious. People who don't know Jesus should be plainly told about their Savior. Why is that confusing? Why did I scheme? Why did I plan? Why did I manipulate? Why did I devise?

I considered my own loneliness and how it might have contributed to this missed opportunity. The word that kept flashing in my brain like a neon sign was BELONG. Is belonging the opposite of loneliness? Do we have a word for that?

I missed this opportunity to speak a deeper truth because I wanted to BELONG. And I don't think that is an ignoble thing. After all, God wants us to belong, too. But He wants for us a Godly belonging, where we belong to each other, all together, interconnected, neighbors-like-selves, everyone. God came for everyone.

In my loneliness, I took a shortcut to belonging.

For a moment, I felt included and part of a mission. I was thankful for the camaraderie of the club. I jumped on board and threw my arms around these girls, *these girls only*, missing a much bigger picture. I realized that these chaplains probably felt the exact same way that I did. They were probably a little bit lonely, or maybe even a lot, but they were thankful to be part of something. They were appreciative of the cohorts, ready to give what was needed to those who were needy. But all the while, often from our desire to belong, we separate ourselves from that title, The Needy, the "crazies," the *other*.

It's a shortcut to belonging, isn't it?

It's not the kind of belonging that God calls for.

It's too small.

It's too easy.

It's not True.

Our titles and artificial groups might temporarily fix our loneliness, but so often our desire to align ourselves with something forms boundaries where none were intended. We distance ourselves from "others," those "crazies," by creating names for them, by putting them in a group all by their lonesome. We marginalize them as being the group that needs ministering to especially, and then make ourselves feel better by believing we are part of a more desirable group. When we do that, don't we remove ourselves from that table to which we desperately want to be invited?

Jesus would have received the Pharisees the same way that He received the outcasts. He would have. But the Pharisees had trouble with how He received the outcasts. The Pharisees had given themselves a special name, an important group, membership in the desirable club. And the rest? Well, they were a little "crazy." And "crazy" wasn't quite good enough. The "crazies" were in need. And the Pharisees weren't.

A couple of days later, I read a parable from Jesus in Matthew 13:24-30 about a man who sowed seed in his field. It was good seed, the story goes. But an enemy came while all were asleep and littered the field with weeds. The owner's steadfast servants came to him and asked, "Sir, did you not sow good seed in your field? How then does it have [weeds]?" (Matthew 13:27)

The owner explained that an enemy was responsible.

So very steadfast, the servants asked if he wanted them to go ahead and get rid of the problem.

"But he said, 'No; for while you are gathering up the tares, you may uproot the wheat with them. Allow both to grow together until the harvest; and in the time of the harvest I will say to the reapers, "First gather up the tares and bind them in bundles to burn them up; but gather the wheat into my barn.'''" (Matthew 13:29-30)

I love it when God's Word thumps me in the forehead. It is my favorite way that He shows up. God tries to put it so plainly for me! I need thumps sometimes. Right in the forehead.

The well-meaning servant plainly points out, "God. I see we have some suspect wheat here."

"You're right about that," God says.

"Want me to separate it out?" he asks trying to be helpful.

"Nope. No offense, but you're not that great at it. You'll make mistakes. Let's just leave that up to someone else. In the meantime just grow together, kid."

Isn't this just great?! I think it should be on t-shirts and billboards. *Thanks, but no thanks. You suck at separating. Concentrate on growing instead. Love, God.*

When it comes to separating, our strengths lie elsewhere. It's just not our bag. God welcomes those we usually reject. God chooses those we would pass over. God puts to work those we would fire. God befriends those we would leave out. We are bad at it, He says. It's just not our job, He says.

We can't go around drawing definitive, decisive lines, putting people in piles. He doesn't mince words about that. The elite didn't like being in the same pile as the "crazies." They refused to grow together. They insisted on separate piles. They liked their ostracizing lines so much that they missed God when He was right there among them inviting everyone to the same table. There is only one table.

We can't miss God because we like our group!

We long to belong, but there are better, truer ways to do it.

We can't make Godly decisions, that are not ours to make, based on our desire to fit in.

I did that.

And I led a group of precious, well-meaning girls to do the same.

I know that I am one of those "crazies," but the world probably sees me as a chaplain. A part of me longs to be covered in tattoos, but in reality I am covered in spit up. And no matter which camp I fit into more neatly, I make mistakes. We all do. That's the point, isn't it? We *all* do. We are all in the same pile. Together. There is only one table. And separation is not for us.

Those "crazies" wish to find a wild ride and miss. Those chaplains wish to change those "crazies" and miss. I wish to mentor those chaplains and miss. We miss. It's what we do. It's who we are. And the way that we miss just doesn't matter, does it? God embraces us all as His very own and covers our misses with endless grace, if we let Him.

Let us grow together.

"There is neither Jew nor Greek, there is neither slave nor free man, there is no male and female, for you are all one in Christ Jesus." (Galatians 3:28)

TO CONSIDER:

1. Are there parts of your personality that pull at each other? How would you like to be perceived?
2. Have you ever misunderstood Jesus and then misrepresented Him? Or, have you ever been on the receiving end of misguided ministry?
3. Has loneliness or insecurity ever directly caused a misstep? Be specific.
4. Where do you draw your separating lines? At what point are you uncomfortable "growing together?" Is that point found outside your country? Your religion? Your denomination? Your socioeconomic class? Your race? Etc.

TO PRACTICE:

Call or email someone outside of your intimate circle and make a coffee/ lunch date.

TO LISTEN:

1. "Open Wide" by Future of Forestry
2. "All the Poor and Powerless" by All Sons and Daughters

CHAPTER 6:

Facebook Fights &
Sleepless Nights

*"How is it they live for eons
in such harmony—the billions of stars—
when most men can barely go a minute
without declaring war in their mind
against someone they know."*
—ST. THOMAS AQUINAS

*"Love means to love that which is
unlovable; or it is no virtue at all."*
—G.K. CHESTERTON

T here's controversial stuff in the world—politics, religion, Miley Cyrus—and I don't so much prefer to be in the middle of it. Social tension stresses me out. I physically cannot watch *The Bachelor* or *The Bachelorette* without acrobatics. I flop on the floor. I hide my eyes the whole time. I sweat. I squeal. I stand on my head. I leave the room a jillion times. This is not theatrics, it is *stress*. I can't take it.

The tricky part about this is that even though I hate tension and have Care Bear tendencies, I also have a very strong sense of justice when it comes to standing up for whom I may perceive to be an underdog. It is important to my soul for things to be set right. This combination of intense aversion to conflict, yet intense insistence on *justice*, has had its troubles. You see how they don't quite go together. In real life, I like to think that I tackle things as they come, but on social media, I have found it's best just to stay out of it. So when tensions arise on Facebook, I run for the Google hills and surf the web instead. The last thing 500 of my nearest and dearest need to see are my somersaults and shrieks and death grip on justice. I have been pretty good about staying conflict-free on Facebook.

Except there was that one time. When I. Just. Couldn't. Let. It. GOOOO.

My friend, we shall call her Greta, is this gem of a friend who laughs easily and heartily. She is laughing in every picture she takes. She lives life with a fullness that others envy. She can get along with anyone and has friends of all kinds. You might find her in a biker bar enjoying a cold beer or at a glitzy gala sipping champagne. Whatever the case, she's on the dance floor. If you come up with a harebrained idea, she's the friend that says, "DO it! I'll do it with you!" She lives and speaks with kindness. She isn't one to argue or offend, and is never at the center of drama. In fact, dramatics can be going on all around her and usually someone has to fill her in that there was almost a fistfight. She just doesn't look for trouble. It's not who she is. She is a giver. The poor are near and dear to her heart. She has quit her job before, with no backup plan, to go serve the poor in South America, and volunteered one year of her time without a paycheck to do it. People matter to her.

Greta loves God. She wants to love God. She's trying to love God. But frankly, it's been a slow-going journey. She has taken one step forward and then a couple back, as we all do when accepting something Life Changing—and she's certainly been no stranger to Life Changes. As she's searched and found, she has struggled to find a way to praise Him that suits her. She's not necessarily your mega church, hand clapping, full rock band, pastor in skinny jeans kinda church girl. But she's hardly your traditional, dusty hymn, old organ kind of celebrator either. She's more of a sunset while hiking, giving books to kids who have none, laughing around a table kind of praiser. While faith has not come easily, she is searching and curious and looks for Him along her way.

Greta's mom passed away when we were 21.

Greta's dad remarried when we were 33.

The woman whom Greta's dad married—we shall call her Diane—is a conservative, Southern Baptist with strong political views, militant moral convictions, and a very loud voice. *I do not think there is one thing wrong with any of those descriptors,* but they are hardly the ones that I would use to describe Greta. Let's just say that if Greta and Diane were on match.com, they would filter each other out.

The ways that people are different from Greta endear them to her. She is intrigued. Respectfully intrigued. However, there are several ways that Diane has been *less endeared* by some of Greta's quirks and decisions, and so Greta's respectful intrigue isn't quite mutual, it has seemed. Diane has been a bit of a bull in a china shop. And Greta has had to grieve many, many fine figurines that Diane has broken while running and yelling through the tender, vulnerable aisles of the You Married My Dad And I Really Wish My Mom Were Still Here Store.

Despite the figurines, Greta loves people. And she's an optimist. This is an excellent recipe for forgiveness and peace.

But it is not foolproof.

On Good Friday a couple of years ago, Greta, with what was for her a very bold move, celebrated Good Friday with a Facebook post that said this: Jesus was a liberal, social worker, hippy who loved people. Now that's a God I can get behind. Happy Good Friday, everyone. God bless!

I hadn't yet seen this post, but as I logged onto Facebook, I received an instant message from Greta asking if I had seen her post. I answered quickly that I had not. She instructed me to go to her page. And then she told me she was so mad that her hands were shaking and tears were involuntarily springing from her eyes. Quickly I punched in her name. I read the post and smiled heartily that Greta had found a way to identify with Jesus. I wanted to quickly affirm her before I looked for what could have made her so upset. I really felt like her naming Jesus on her page and celebrating what He had done for her *had* to be more important than what was going on. So I took two seconds to type in, "that hippy is a fool for you," or something like that, and then sifted through the comments to look for anything offensive. And there it was.

Diane.

Diane loud and proud.

The first to comment, she said this: *No liberal, hippy, social worker would EVER willingly put themselves on a cross and die for you. Jesus Christ is the world's only Savior, God's one son, and my personal Lord, and He was none of those things.*

OK.

Now *my* hands were shaking as I tried to figure out the best way to take up for my friend who had made herself vulnerable perhaps for the first time in God's name. I would NOT have her suffer because of it. I could not.

I decided to turn to Scripture. The verse that immediately came to mind was the one where Paul said that he had put aside his rights, removed cultural barriers, and set aside nonmoral issues in order to become all things to all men. I thought this was *perfect* and Diane, as a firm believer undoubtedly trying to win people to Christ, should heed his advice and chill the heck out. After all, I thought the verse did a great job of explaining how two *very different* people can find the *exact same* man intensely lovable because he became a slave to all. Jesus wanted to save *everyone*. So I found the verse:

"For though I am free from all men, I have made myself a slave to all, so that I may win more. To the Jews I became as a Jew, so that I might win Jews; to those who are under the Law, as under the Law though not being myself under the Law, so that I might win those who are under the Law; to those who are without law, as without law, though not being without the law of God but under the law of Christ, so that I might win those who are without law. To the weak I became weak, that I might win the weak; I have become all things to all men, so that I may by all means save some. I do all things for the sake of the gospel, so that I may become a fellow partaker of it." (1 Corinthians 9:19-23)

I punched it in as quickly as I could. I couldn't push post fast enough because I was pretty certain that Paul had written that part of the Bible just for Greta and just for Diane, just for this very day. And then I waited for the likes to start rolling in. Which they did. For other commenters to come to Greta's rescue. Which they did. I reread Diane's comment. I reread my comment. And then, after not near enough discernment, I decided that God's Word needed my help. Of course it did. Indeed. Diane probably couldn't read. So she needed me not only to share the verse, but most certainly she also needed my interpretation of it. God's words weren't nearly enough. Nope. Decidedly, I needed to interject some of my own.

So....

An addendum: *Diane, when people put God in a box they will always be larger than Him. And it seems to me that you are mighty large and your God is mighty small. God isn't just for you.*

I pushed post and smiled, pleased with myself. She was so arrogant, that Diane, to spout her opinions all over Facebook that way. She had hurt my vulnerable friend trying to find her way. I couldn't think of a bigger barrier to accepting Christianity than what Diane had just done. I knew my comment wasn't nice, but considering the potential damage this woman was causing I felt very, very justified. There needed to be another voice and I had nominated myself. This needed to be set right.

Sadly, I decided I wasn't finished.

I went on: *Diane, your Savior you speak of commands you to love your neighbor. And guess what? Your neighbor is everyone. The hippy. The liberal. The social worker. Not the people just like you. Because that's too easy, Diane.*

Fine. Good. There. I was done.

But wait, one more thing: *Diane, you might very well be dutiful, but you are not compassionate. And, I suspect your halo might be on just a bit too tight.*

I felt excellent about all of this. Excellent, I tell you. There was my sad, shaking friend, now justified. Because of me, my friend—a precious person to whom faith has not come easy—could see what real faith looked like. Curtsy.

Everything was great until I tried to go to sleep that night, but kept hearing this: Maybe, just maybe, I am missing Jesus' point. I might be missing Jesus' point if I am using His words to hurt people. Maybe. Probably. Definitely. Darn.

And then I heard this: "For though I am free from all men, I have made myself a slave to **all**, so that I may win more." (**emphasis mine**) (1 Corinthians 9:19)

And this: *Allison, God isn't just for* ***you***.

And this: *Allison, your Savior you speak of commands you to love your neighbor. And guess what? Your neighbor is everyone. Not just the people just like* **you**. *Because that's too easy,* **Allison**.

And one more: **Allison**, *you might very well be dutiful, but you are not compassionate. And, I suspect your halo might be on too tight.*

Nice.

I tossed and I turned and I grappled and I complained before realizing that I had this lesson to learn: Love does not mean standing up for the poor in spirit and turning on those who are not so meek. Love is learning that God loves Greta intensely and He loves Diane *just as much.* For that reason only, it is my job also to work to find both of them delightful. Yes, it's easier for me to find Greta delightful. But even jerks are good to people whom they enjoy. So how I treat difficult people who, with their challenging personality types, burrow under my skin, how I treat Diane—shouldn't that say more about me? Wouldn't responding to Diane with a gentle rebuke, or refraining from discussing the size of her halo, or simply praising Greta, or posting God's word and then *leaving it alone*—wouldn't that shine a brighter light on whom my God is and how I understand Him? Being a peacemaker, not a peacetaker, involves finding the God in everyone and having patience and compassion for the parts that aren't yet Godly, including my own.

To be fair, I thought I was fighting for peace. I know, it seems silly now, that little oxymoron. I discovered that peace isn't fighting for what we believe to be right, winning, and then settling in to the feeling of having been justified like it is a cozy sweater. A sneaky Enemy would have us think that is the exact definition of peace —fighting, winning, and then being justified. Believing that, I took all of my unrighteous wrath and put it towards Diane one day, showing the world only that I was exactly like her—the other direction—but exactly like her. In my mind, I delivered justice. In her mind, she delivered justice. *But it isn't ours to deliver.* It is God's. And He will. When He chooses. And He is far more patient than we are.

Our job is to show kindness and compassion because we ourselves have been shown so much.

* * *

After the Facebook debacle, Greta tried to reach out to Diane to let her know how hurt she was and Diane never responded to her email. Miraculously, they have found a way to be together for short periods of time that are not harmful. I am amazed by Greta's capacity for forgiveness. Truly. I, myself, had not been harmed and yet I could feel rage in my chest when I thought of how offensive Diane had been. Greta's peace in the midst of so many hurt feelings made me analyze my lack of it in more personal areas of my life, and I came to something life changing.

Our Christian life is about life as part of a Body. Our faith-life is not limited just to ourselves and the Lord. We live in community and we oftentimes run into each other leaving bumps and bruises. We all have a story that will break your heart. I know firsthand how bitterness can gnaw, rage can churn, and angry thoughts can pile up until there isn't room for much else. I know about that clutching emotion that robs us of sleep as we rehearse conversations where we are eloquently victorious, thinking of clever ways to tell off the people who hurt us. Tossing and turning and delivering justice with our sharp tongues and excellent points—yes, I know that feeling.

And yet, I have been given infinite amounts of mercy.

Is justice what I want? Really?

But what do we do with the person who may never, ever be sorry? What do we do with the person who may never care to acknowledge our bruises and bumps? Because that's the assignment, isn't it?

Just like it is easy to extend all of our compassion to those whom we enjoy, it is also easy and wondrous and enjoyable to extend grace to those who ask for it. That's simple! Fun, even! But what about those who don't? What do we do then?

We must give mercy.

Has Jesus asked us to do something impossible? For a while, I thought that He had. As I examined my own personal bumps and bruises, my own "Diane", I realized how much work I still had to do when it came to the forgiveness that we have been called to give. Because I would lie awake at night begging for peace, begging for forgiveness to enter my heart, to wash it clean, but no matter what I did or how hard I prayed, I couldn't will it to come. I longed for my harsh feelings to loosen their grip, but the turmoil wouldn't let up. I yearned for my heart to feel what my mind knew that it should, but it wasn't cooperating no matter how hard I tried. There were many sleepless nights.

I did the things I knew to do. I prayed. I prayed hard. I prayed for these people who had hurt me and didn't seem to care. I prayed intensely for their blessings. I had running lists of the peace I tried to hope that they felt, the prosperity that they would experience, the friends who would help them celebrate life.

I had tricks. When I taught middle school, some of my students were so unruly that I sometimes felt the urge to kick them in the shin. Because I needed a job and because I loved Jesus, I knew I needed to come up with a plan to love them better or at least not assault a minor. What I came up with was picturing them asleep. What would they be wearing? What would their breathing sound like? In what position had their body finally (finally!) relaxed for the day? I softened with compassion thinking of them so vulnerable, so peaceful.

So I practiced this with the people who had hurt me. I pictured them as young children with chubby hands and big dreams and wearing tutus and speaking with a lisp, desperately hoping that the image of them in their youth would dissolve any pain they had caused me in their adulthood. In my yoga practice, I pictured physically breathing for them hoping with all my might that us being in rhythm together, needing one another, might loosen something locked. I'm sure that my tricks were useful. I do not think that any of that was a waste of time, but it wasn't until I made two revelations that something shifted my heart and it finally clicked in sync with my mind.

In my life, I could clearly see the two reasons why I was clinging to justice and wasn't forgiving with the enthusiasm that I was called to give.

The first reason is that I didn't realize how large my own debt was.

And the second reason is that I thought I could chip away at my debt until I was free.

Those two misconceptions greatly, greatly hindered how I felt about someone whom I thought owed me something. I mistakenly thought I was in charge of other people's debt, when I am only in charge of my own—and even then, minimally so.

In Matthew 18:21-35, Peter asks Jesus how many times he has to forgive the same person (I adore Peter), and here is what Jesus has to say about it. Sadly, the unmerciful servant and I have a few things in common.

"Jesus said to him, 'I do not say to you, up to seven times, but up to seventy times seven.'" (Matthew 18:22)

Then Jesus goes on to tell a story about a king who wanted to settle up with his slaves. In the mix was a slave who owed ten thousand talents, and due to the great amount, he was completely incapable of ever paying it back. The king commanded that the slave and his family be sold. The slave fell on his face, begged for mercy, and promised to pay him back. The king felt compassion and quickly forgave his debt.

After that, the slave went and found a colleague who owed him money, just a hundred denarii. This was pennies compared to what the slave previously owed the king, but the slave began to choke his colleague demanding proper payment. The fellow debtor fell on his face and begged for mercy, but the slave gave him no mercy and had him thrown into prison instead.

When the king heard about this, he said, "'You wicked slave, I forgave you all that debt because you pleaded with me. Should you not also have had mercy on your fellow slave, in the same way that I had mercy on you?'" (Matthew 18:32-33) And the rest of the story didn't turn out so well for the slave who was given much and refused to return the favor.

Here it was clear that I, myself, owe ten thousand talents to my Master!

People disagree about how much money that translates to, but everyone agrees that it is an amount that this servant could have never, ever paid off. I am in debt. And I can never do anything about it except to accept the absolution and be eternally grateful. And frankly, I had become used to my gift. I wasn't celebrating anymore. I had grown accustomed to the kindness. I walked around my life seeking justice in the obvious places, pennies in comparison to the millions I owed, forgetting that I, myself, hadn't been treated with justice at all! The better we understand that we are forgiven, the better we can forgive others. I had forgotten my debt.

The other thing that was turning me inside out was that my adversary's behavior wasn't changing. I realized that in my circumstance, I was expected to just move peacefully along. Working on the same committee, week after week, we were forced to work collaboratively on an important group project, and the expectation was to show up, forget about any offenses, and get the job done. But I couldn't do it because I had a death grip on justice. The lack of acknowledgment of my experience, my feelings, my excellent points frustrated me fiercely. But I finally allowed His Word to teach me that we forgive wrongly when we hold on to debt and imply that people must change in order to work off any grievance.

I thought that my forgiveness equaled their kindness.

But delivering mercy is not the same thing as a negotiating a trade. True forgiveness is not making an exchange. True forgiveness is a gift. Denarii to the talent, pennies to the dollar, a tiny representation of what is ours, the least that we could do.

My first mistake was thinking that I could repay the kindness of God by being dutiful. Tit for tat was a terribly wrong mindset that permeated every relationship that I was in.

See, I put myself in a situation with God where we did favors for one another, like old pals, greatly overestimating my abilities and ignoring the gospel altogether. That attitude led me to believe that people were to pay back what they owed. Fundamentally, I held on far too tightly to the belief that kind people should carry remorse when they hurt someone, and change their behavior in future situations, and only then would justice be served as they chipped away at their debt, earning a good relationship. Frankly, I thought I had to earn God's respect through my dutiful life and I looked down on others who didn't seem to be trying nearly as hard as I was at being kind to others.

My mercy was contingent on good behavior.

But our Lord's is not.

The servant in this parable was never expected to return any favor! That is a ludicrous notion. He could never do that! For one, thinking that my own payment was possible meant that I didn't understand the grandness of what I had been given. And two, that erroneous belief kept me expecting the same payment from others.

These two realizations changed everything. I was free. I wasn't free because I didn't remember the hurt. I wasn't free because I changed my mind about my situation. I wasn't free because I wanted to have slumber parties, and shopping Saturdays with my colleagues. I was free because my heart had changed. I was free because I now truly desired those things for which I made myself pray. I was free because I finally understood my role. And it had nothing—absolutely nothing—to do with justice. That was for Him. My only job was to hand out what I had been given in abundance. My debt was so great and there was absolutely no chance at making it right, so my only option was to pour mercy out lavishly on others regardless of their own personal red ink. Their red ink just wasn't my business. I had my own.

So what are we to do with the people in our lives who will never be sorry? We give them mercy. Mercy without expectation. There are no contingencies. Mercy is not a trade for good behavior. It is a gift. It is forgiven. It is gone. And the next time? Mercy. Mercy without expectation. There are no contingencies. Mercy is not a trade for good behavior. It is a gift. It is forgiven. It is gone. And the next time? Yep, that's right.

Forgiveness is rarely once and for all. We give it over and over. Whenever feelings of injustice rise in our hearts we remember our gift, our gift that we can absolutely do nothing about. Over and over, we give it, knowing that the Lord understands that we are bad at it. We give it 490 times, too many times to count, to the same person, about the same situation, as many times as necessary, knowing that the Lord forgives our rudimentary attempts to love like He does. We give it and ask for His mercy when it is hard to give again and again.

And we find ourselves free.

No late night rehearsed conversations.

No embarrassing exchanges on Facebook. But instead, a heart that knows what our head does—that forgiveness means letting go of our need for things to be set right because in the gospel nothing is set right. The gospel centers around injustice! After all, freedom depends on God attributing Christ's perfect obedience onto us. An immeasurable gift that all we can do is return. Again and again and again.

"Since you have in obedience to the truth purified your souls for a sincere love of the brethren, fervently love one another from the heart...." (1 Peter 1:22)

"You have heard that it was said, 'You shall love your neighbor and hate your enemy.' But I say to you, love your enemies and pray for those who persecute you, so that you may be sons of your Father who is in heaven; for He causes

His sun to rise on the evil and the good, and sends rain on the righteous and the unrighteous. For if you love those who love you, what reward do you have? Do not even the tax collectors do the same? If you greet only your brothers, what more are you doing than others? Do not even the Gentiles do the same? Therefore you are to be perfect, as your heavenly Father is perfect." (Matthew 5:43-48)

To Consider:

1. How has social media affected your confidence? Has it been bolstered or taken a hit? How has social media affected how we relate to each other, or share our opinions? How has it affected how kind or frank we are?

2. Has there ever been a time when God has used your own words to convict you?

3. For which personality types is it easy for you to lend mercy? For which is it more difficult?

4. Have you lived in a way that suggests that mercy is a trade instead of a gift? What does that say about what you may believe about God?

To Practice:

Write a letter to someone you are having a hard time forgiving. Maybe it is just for you, maybe it is to send. Pray for one week about which is the right thing to do.

To Listen:

1. "More Love, Less Attack" by Needtobreathe
2. "By Our Love" by Christy Nockels

SCISSORS

Shedding, Snipping, Gone,

Holiness born of great thanks

for Love You gave first

CHAPTER 7:

Holiness, A Cart Not A Horse

"We have to find a new balance; otherwise even the
moral edifice of the church is likely to fall like a house of
cards, losing the freshness and fragrance of the Gospel.
The proposal of the Gospel must be more simple,
profound, radiant. It is from this proposition that the
moral consequences then flow."
—POPE FRANCIS

I've always wondered what was so repulsive about tax collectors in Jesus' time. I tend to think of them as the modern day used car salesman, but I have a few used cars and I rather enjoyed the people we bought them from. I've never really seen the big deal.

Sure, tax collectors took money, that's annoying, but it was their job. I mean, I don't hate the mail carrier for delivering junk mail, it's just part of the job. But I looked into it. Here's what had people in a tiff.

Rome occupied Palestine. Because of Roman occupation, the Jews were subject to Roman laws, Roman soldiers, and Roman taxes. The Jews were resentful of the Romans' presence—and most especially of their taxes. Essentially, they had to give their hard-earned money to an enemy. What made it worse was that the Romans wanted taxes but they didn't want to use their own people to collect them, so they hired Palestinian locals and told them they could keep a percentage of what they gathered. So the more tax collectors collected, the more money they kept.

Tax collectors betrayed their own people—they were helping an oppressor—and they were thieving to make themselves wealthy. So yeah, they were despised. They were seen as traitors. Very expensive traitors. This made for an awful situation that brought out the worst in everyone. The Romans were bullies, the tax collectors were traitors and thieves, and the rest of the Palestinians were a bitter, hateful bunch toward both.

Zacchaeus was a tax collector who was not going to win any popularity contests in his town of Jericho. The Bible tells us that he was a wealthy man. While he may have been good at his job, it came at his neighbors' expense, and the people in his town detested him.

Jesus, on his way to Jerusalem, stopped in Jericho, and drew a crowd while He was there. The people gathered as he passed through. The Bible tells us that Zacchaeus ran ahead of the crowd to get a good look at Jesus. There's no way to know for sure what Zacchaeus was feeling the day that Jesus came to his town, but we do know that despite being a thieving rascal, he didn't scoff, mock, or ignore this man's holiness. To the contrary, he ran ahead to get a good look and when that didn't work out, he climbed a tree instead.

Can you picture it? Zacchaeus having a hard time seeing, trying to run in front of the crowd, struggling to keep up, jumping up and down just to see. Then, when that did not work, saying to heck with it, separating himself from the crowd, and running for the closest tree and scaling it just to lay eyes on this teacher named Jesus.

There were many in the crowd, but Jesus noticed the guy who was desperate to see.

Jesus had never met Zacchaeus, but called him by name: "Zacchaeus, hurry and come down, for today I must stay at your house." (Luke 19:5)

In a society that specialized in sin management and maintaining outer purity, entering the house of this public sinner was definitely shocking. But never one to pander, Jesus didn't reach out to Zacchaeus in private. In front of many, a disapproving many, Jesus extended grace to Zacchaeus with a warm invitation to share a meal. The Bible tells us that Zacchaeus received Him gladly. This Jesus whom he probably thought was for everyone else, certainly not him, just singled him out to share some private time.

Jesus' invitation was no small gesture. People couldn't believe what they were seeing. The Bible tells us that they began to grumble.

Jesus' invitation came at a cost. And Zacchaeus noticed.

Zacchaeus had gained prosperity by hurting his neighbors. A career of taking what was not his had made him wealthy. But the disdain of a town had not compelled him to do what was right. Not their anger, nor their hatred, nor their ostracizing, nor their preaching, nor their shame compelled Zacchaeus to change. It was one afternoon with Jesus that made it clear to Zacchaeus that he had to choose. In one meal with Jesus, Zacchaeus came to this conclusion: "I give half my belongings, Lord, to the poor. If I have defrauded anyone in the least, I pay him back fourfold." (Luke 19:8).

After receiving the gift of grace, Zacchaeus felt compelled to respond. He felt compelled to empty his pockets and fill his soul. He longed to let go of other people's money. He yearned to search out the poor and right his wrongs.

When Zacchaeus, despite his debauchery, was accepted by Christ, repentance followed and salvation came. Zacchaeus, moved by the kindness of Christ, responded. And this is where we must begin our search for holiness.

What is our response to Christ's kindness?

Of what, do we need to let go?

It might not be other people's money, but what is it that is holding us back? What is it that we should be in search of instead?

* * *

I was the type of student who was way too cool to be a goody goody (banana clips in every color and all the grossest Garbage Pail Kids to prove it) but way too afraid of the wrath of my mom to be a class clown. I had class clown tendencies (I liked attention) but my mom worked at the school. That meant that I was skilled at straddling the line between making well-timed smart aleck comments and stopping at the precise moment before the teacher got so annoyed with me that she threatened to tell my mom. I was a little wild at heart, but fear, not necessarily respect for the rules, always reined it in.

I almost dropped out of the third grade over long division. My teacher was Mrs. Pett and I thought carrying, and rounding, and the tens place were going to be the end of my scholastic career. And honestly I was fine with it. I had decided that any career involving math would leave me gray, grumpy and disgruntled anyway, and if school was just preparing me for that, then I was better off without it. If worse came to worst, I decided, I could always be Jack Hannah's cute assistant in a banana clip or a rodeo clown. There was no long division involved. I checked.

One day during a long division quiz, Mrs. Pett caught me looking at Christian Jessup's paper. Christian Jessup was really good at hawking loogies and even better at long division. I wasn't cheating necessarily. I was just, you know, checking my answer. Innocent almost because it wasn't like I hadn't done the work. I suppose some really goody goody circles would call that cheating, but here's the deal—I was a nice person. I was a good kid. A little mouthy, but mostly decent, and well, long division made me erase holes in my paper and try out new cuss words I had learned on the bus. I wasn't this cheater who I appeared to be. I wasn't! It had just been a long year. And we had just finished our fractions unit. And I was so bad at fractions that I had missed approximately 5/8ths of last month's recesses staying inside to stare at pies trying desperately to guess the right amount to shade. I needed this answer, that was all.

I knew in my bones that there was absolutely no way that Mrs. Pett would see things the same as me. I was doomed. I just knew it. After all, for the pleasure of my classmates, I had spent the whole year perfecting her accent so I could make fun of her behind her back while she wrote on the chalkboard. Not that it matters, but my impersonation was spot on, if I do say so myself.

But do you know what Mrs. Pett did when she saw me looking at Christian's paper?

She winked at me.

And then went back to grading her papers.

I thought for certain she would yank me up by my puff painted shirt and drag me to the principal or worse, to my mom, but instead she looked past my crime and right into my heart and winked at me.

I think in that moment Mrs. Pett saw that there was something inside of me, despite my sharp tongue and annoying attention-seeking tendencies, that longed to be good at long division... even though I wasn't. Even though I had the wrong answer, I yearned for the right one.

Similarly, there was something inside of Zacchaeus, despite his sneaky, thieving ways, that longed to have it all... even though he didn't. Even though he couldn't see, he yearned for a good look. And Jesus Christ looked to the top of a tree and gave him a wink.

Zacchaeus responded in holiness.

It was right then and there, after Ms. Pett winked at me and then went back to grading her papers, that I became a goody goody. *Yes ma'ams* and *yes pleases* and *how can I helps* peppered my conversations with Mrs. Pett. I never spent any more energy thinking up clever nicknames for her. I was right on time and first in line. Out of a new respect for Mrs. Pett, I longed to please her. She had shown me grace. And she just didn't have to do that.

My new goody goody tendencies—were they fashionable? No, not really. I suffered a little for it. But I didn't care. I only answered to Mrs. Pett now. I would have done anything for another of those winks.

Before the Long Division/Winking Incident of 1985, I looked around at all of those goody goodies and felt nothing but pity for all of their longsuffering. Compliance seemed like such a bore. But now? Now?! Compliance was all my pleasure! Compliance was a joy. Before I received grace, I understood obedience as a chore, a very laborious chore, instead of a *response*, a very eager *response*. Zaccheaus and Mrs. Pett helped me see that I had holiness all wrong, and it was because I hadn't yet recognized the kindness of Christ—His grace preceding my every holy endeavor. My *gratefulness* leading to my holiness, my holiness leading to my *freedom*.

Last year, in a Bible Study that I lead, I asked the college girls who attended it to tell me what they thought of when they heard the word *holy*. Here's what they said: serious, harsh, boring, problem free, guilt free, white, sacrificial, lonely, healed. I could see that mixed in with some truth was a whole lot of hardship. Apparently I wasn't the only one who thought obedience was drudgery. I related to their confining definition.

In essence, it was in the third grade that I was exposed to what true holiness was, and because I'm as good at holiness as I am at long division, it wasn't until embarrassingly late that I generalized the concept to my Christian walk. I am still working everyday. The concept I've finally got, but the rounding and the carrying and the tens place, that's a different story. We've got to commit to something though! In response to the kindness of Christ, Zacchaeus committed to giving up a few things and going in search of some other things. That was his committed response to the gift of grace.

* * *

Understanding that holiness is for my benefit and transformation, and not my boredom and incarceration, is still a challenging concept to grasp. Throughout much of my early Christian life, I focused on my own holy efforts—my increased knowledge, my meditations, my good attendance, my doings, my undoings. After all, God tells us over and over that He wants us holy. He wants us to embrace what is right over what is wrong. I thought I was doing a pretty darn good job.

I knew that I was *to pursue righteousness, to abstain from every evil, to consecrate myself and be holy, to walk properly, to glorify God in my body, to be an imitator of God, to be holy because He is holy, to go and sin no more.* (Proverbs 21:21, 1 Thessalonians 5:22, Leviticus 20:7, Romans 13:12-14, 1 Corinthians 6:20, Ephesians 5:1, Leviticus 11:45, John 8:11)

Holiness mattered. He couldn't make it any clearer. Consequently, I spent my time focusing on holiness. But it did not go very well. One failure after another—it did not go well. My self-discipline only got me so far. I was missing something.

And this something was important. It was paramount. And it occurred to me as I read the parable of the barren fig tree (Luke 13:6-9).

In this story there is a vineyard owner who represents God. He inspects his vineyard and finds a barren fig tree despite three whole years of looking for fruit. He orders the tree with no fruit to be cut down because as it is, it is only taking up space. But the gardener who represents Jesus pleads for a little more time. He intercedes on behalf of Israel, on behalf of the individual to please allow Him to tend to the tree with more care, more fertilizer. Jesus, who feeds his people and gives them Living Water, asks for an extension and mercifully, the Lord who had every right to cut down the tree, grants the request by responding with patience.

It is obvious from this parable that fruit is expected. And the Lord is waiting.

Right, I knew that.

But.

The motivation to transform is the love that He gave first.

It must start there!

Concentrating on my own holy efforts resulted in failure. My self-discipline always failed, regularly ran out, repeatedly gave up. But His love could never! I was laser focused on *my* performance instead of *His* great love, and once I made the shift, holiness was about nothing less than gratitude.

And if holiness does not start from gratitude, then I am inclined to believe that it is no longer holy.

If, at the root of our holy efforts, is some desire to keep up or ascend or pose or compensate, it is not holiness but has become something else.

God's grace is given with the hope that it will be a catalyst for transformation. The hope is that God's kindness will transform us and draw us to repentance. Zacchaeus understood this.

I thought about Zacchaeus. And then I thought about Jesus' large audience as he discussed the fig tree, which surely included the Pharisees. To Zacchaeus, salvation came, but the Pharisees were referred to as evildoers.

Both parties, Zacchaeus and the Pharisees, were working in the name of the Lord, were they not? But Jesus did not look on their efforts equally. Like Zacchaeus, the Pharisees were certainly working hard. But was it holy?

In which camp did I fall? Were my holy efforts like those of Zacchaeus or were they something different? This answer mattered.

Zacchaeus separated himself from the crowd by making an effort to get a good look. He accepted Jesus' invitation. He appreciated the kindness of Christ and was moved to repentance. He was transformed. The Pharisees, on the other hand, separated themselves from the crowd predominantly for self-serving purposes. They seemed to miss acceptance, appreciation, and transformation all together.

What's important is that the kindness of Christ was lost on the Pharisees.

They didn't understand this Jesus just yet, and what He offered was something they didn't think that they needed. The Pharisees were confused. Jesus didn't look how they thought He might. He didn't care about the matters that they thought He would. He didn't treat people the way that they expected Him to. They insisted that He obey their systems, and their systems didn't allow for lunch with losers. So they grumbled instead of cheered. They were confused.

There is something about confusion that doesn't elicit our best response.

And they missed a moment. Their Lord was right alongside them and they missed it.

Similarly, I previously had read the parable of the barren fig tree and only heard the message about fruit. I saw the seriousness of the call. And I banged out some service projects. I focused on the destruction of that tree while failing to notice the nurture of that tree.

Thankfully, the Holy Spirit has since taught me that my initial focus settled in the wrong place. I should have rested on the care that I have been given and the kind negotiating on my behalf.

I'm guessing here, but perhaps that's where the Pharisees got off track as well. They heard about the destruction of trees and vowed not to tolerate sinful behavior. They vowed never to excuse unrepentant sin. They vowed to bear fruit and simply skipped over the loving details, the extra time and concern they had been given. They forgot about all of that negotiating on their behalf. They weren't moved by it. They were moved by something else.

Perhaps they focused on the threat of destruction instead of the promise of great nurturing. Perhaps they operated from fear instead of gratefulness. I could certainly understand that. Perhaps the Pharisees, like me, got right to work producing and had the misguided thought that they were saving themselves from something terrible. I can see how they ended up pretty impressed with their efforts without understanding that fruit from the wrong source isn't fruit at all. I can see how they muddied all that Living Water.

Real fruit springs from an interaction with the grace of God. Real fruit emerges when we look around and notice the good soil we have been given, the consistent water, the tireless pruning. Real fruit blossoms when we put thanks in the right place. Our works become a result of our gratitude, and our service stems from an overflow of love.

The biggest difference between Zacchaeus and the Pharisees is the heart behind their holiness, a heart spurred on by thanks.

I reflect upon my ignorant thoughts of my goody goody classmates and remember the burden I attached to their obedience. I think about my Bible Study's definition of holiness, and how it encompassed a whole lot of hardship. Holiness without the proper motivation is certainly a chore. But when holiness springs from gratitude, it is freeing, healing, and relieving. It is joy. And that is what Christ wants for us. Not burdens that keep us from him. But good works that tie us to Him.

Obedience isn't drudgery.

It is *worship*.

It is *fruitful*.

He wants us to go in search of holiness because holiness is freedom and He loves us. But an interaction with the grace God must come first.

God wants us healed. God wants us whole. God wants us holy.

* * *

The most tangible and microcosmic example of this happened a couple of years ago while I was staffing a retreat.

The retreat was for kids going off to college and the purpose was to help solidify their faith before they were thrown into the big, bad world full of frat parties and new age professors and void of nagging parents and hovering youth ministers.

The retreat started off peculiarly.

The teenagers rode a bus to the middle of nowhere, which was normal. But once they arrived, they were greeted by strangers. No one looked familiar. And this wasn't the cheery, campy, enthusiastic reception they had come to know. In fact, everyone in charge was stoic and solemn, even a little scary, as the spokesperson giving directions was streaked in black paint. I, as a simple volunteer who was not in charge, was able to perfectly spectate the teens' confusion. The furrowed brows, the darting eyes to see how their peers were responding, the fear, the compensating nonchalance. As they stepped off the bus, they were met by an adult who quickly blindfolded them and led them astray in the dark. Their surroundings similar to an obstacle course, each teenager held on to their assigned adult for guidance, listened keenly to specific instructions: "Duck down," "Further," "Further still." Alarms would sound, surprising them. Some of them clutched the adult with sweaty hands and white knuckles. Some of them giggled their way through. Some of them trembled in the adult's arms. Still others were completely uncommunicative, restrained, made mute.

It was a very confusing Friday night.

After a long night of blindness, their blindfolds were removed and they were led to a place at the table of the Last Supper. As regular participants in their youth group and Bible study, they recognized the table immediately for what it was, but they were tired and confused.

And there is something about confusion that just doesn't elicit our best response.

The room was dark. There was room for thirteen at a time at the table. Bread and wine were placed in the center of it. The character of Jesus was there. Without words, he circled the room and washed their feet. But it had been a long night, so they giggled and rolled their eyes as he knelt down offering himself.

I have often thought about that historic Thursday night before Friday and pondered the disciples' responses to Jesus at His time of greatest need. I mean really, Peter? Three whole times? Your best friend? Before He died? I'm not trying to be judgy or anything, but really, conviction didn't set in after the first or second denial? Or, really guys? You just fell asleep? Your friend is crying in prayer literally sweating blood and you just took a little snooze? You were tired? In the garden? The world's greatest grief? Jesus grieved it alone? Nice work.

But there was something about watching these teenagers miss a moment that helped me understand Jesus' friends that night. I wholeheartedly related to these kids. I could so easily put myself in their position. I wondered if I would have been a giggler or an eye roller when the kindness of Christ knelt at my feet. Their shallow responses, I understood them. They just didn't get it. Not yet.

And the disciples, they were confused. They didn't know what was going on. Their best friend was saying weird things. They couldn't wrap their minds around what He was saying. If they would have known what was to come, that this was their time to prove once and for all what discipleship really looked like, what Jesus' love deserved, if they would have known that this night was their last chance to love Him, well, they would have done it, loved Him so very well.

Hindsight. No confusion.

They would have done it.

And they eventually did. Every single one of them. Because of an empty-tombed Sunday, a heart wrenching Friday wasn't their last chance. They had chance after chance after chance. And besides Judas, every single one of them died a martyr. If there is no other reason to believe in God, it might be that one. Every single one of His best friends (except for one who survived a poison attempt and died of old age in exile) willingly suffered gruesome deaths rather than renounce Him one more time.

The rest of the retreat centered around the kindness of Christ and told of His great love for them. There was the hope that these kids would move away to college and be motivated to follow Him, not in order to keep up, or fit in, or because they might suffer great consequences otherwise, but instead just for the purity of the reason that He loved them first. The retreat focused on what *He* gave, not what *they* needed to give. Hopefully their service would be a beautiful byproduct based off of overflow, but... first things first. Do you understand how He loves you? No, do you? Because it's only then that we can talk about how we can love Him back. Where can we go from there? What we can do? Not to *gain* love, but to *give* it. Because He gave it first.

As we debriefed the retreat in a large group, asking the kids to describe their emotions as they arrived and were led astray, they made beautiful connections about the symbolism of being somewhere unfamiliar and their knee-jerk reactions to strangeness. They dived into the conversation admitting how they clutched or cussed the one leading them, the one they deemed responsible for all of this nonsense. It was enlightening to them. One girl shared that while she was blind and uncomfortable, the only thing she knew to do was pray. Another sweetheart humbly admitted that it never even crossed her mind to pray. She laughed and cried at the same time and told us that she was simply focused on survival. She laughed because she realized how silly it seemed that being blindfolded made her feel like she might die at her high school retreat, and she cried because in a survival situation it slipped her mind to pray. They were learning things about themselves.

As our conversation turned to the Last Supper, and their participation in that portion of the night, the room turned quiet. After a powerful weekend learning about great, great love, it now felt pretty crude that it had started off with giggling and eye rolling. Their eyes turned downward. Offhandedly, the leader of the retreat joked that we had a video camera in the room and would be watching the footage together now. He was joking, of course, but as he said it, their panicked eyes shot up from the floor. The color practically drained from their faces in horror. In shame. They were sorry. They wanted another chance. They wanted another chance to love Him well.

This is what precedes true holiness. A new recognition of what has been offered!

Answering an invitation shouted to the top of a tree, being pardoned by a wink from a teacher's desk, or given new life from death on a cross, we use our lives to say *thank you* instead of *there, that oughta do it*. Humbled by the graciousness of an unpopular decision to hang out at a flashy sinner's house, the kindness to pardon an unruly student, or the selflessness to sacrifice a perfect life so that we might live, we right our wrongs to love Him back because, well, He just didn't have to do that.

Christ offers so much more than just a ticket to heaven. There are glories that He wants for us here on Earth. He has told us over and over where freedoms lie: they are found in our pursuit of earthly holiness.

Holiness isn't boring. It is freeing. But only if we're not confused about why we're doing it.

Jesus has told us that our most fundamental problems stem from within, so it comes as no surprise that holiness is only holy with a right, loving heart. So important are our hearts that I think it is safe to say that lack of holiness is borne of forgetting or ignoring Christ's kindness. We can't be holy by producing, doing, and acting ourselves into a new way of being. Instead, holiness is a gift that God graciously implants within the core of those who have accepted Christ's invitation with the same glad heart as Zacchaeus. Holiness is the holiness of God within us, our efforts revealing our hearts, so that when we walk by the Spirit we will bear fruit. May His great gifts excite us to live how He tells us to, knowing that holiness means freedom.

"Therefore I urge you, brethren, by the mercies of God, to present your bodies a living and holy sacrifice, acceptable to God, which is your spiritual service of **worship**. *And do not be conformed to this world, but be transformed by the renewing of your mind, so that you may prove what the will of God is, that which is good and acceptable and perfect."* **(emphasis mine)** *(Romans 12:1-2)*

To Consider:

1. Have you ever felt that Jesus was for other people, but not for you? Describe your thoughts and feelings. Have you received Him gladly?

2. Has there ever been a time that you have experienced unexpected grace? When was it? How did it make you feel?

3. What do you need to give up? What do you need to go in search of instead?

4. How does fear/intimidation affect the pursuit of holiness? What is it that is at the root of your noble acts or holy efforts?

To Practice:

For one month set aside time to read through the gospels over and over. As you do, make mental notes of Christ's kindness.

To Listen:

1. "Hopeless Wanderer" by Mumford and Sons
2. "Garden" by Needtobreathe

CHAPTER 8:

Moldy Mugs & A Mentee Named Monica

"To love at all is to be vulnerable. Love anything and your heart will be wrung and possibly broken. If you want to make sure of keeping it intact you must give it to no one, not even an animal. Wrap it carefully round with hobbies and little luxuries; avoid all entanglements. Lock it up safe in the casket or coffin of your selfishness. But in that casket, safe, dark, motionless, airless, it will change. It will not be broken; it will become unbreakable, impenetrable, irredeemable. To love is to be vulnerable."
—C.S. LEWIS

One of the most beautiful books I have ever read is *Life of Pi* by Yann Martel. I read it while traveling in Malaysia with two of my best girlfriends. The first night in our hotel, I found one part of it particularly beautiful so I read it out loud to my travel companions. When I finished the passage, they said, "Keep going!" and consequently I read the entire book aloud to my girlfriends on Malay porches, hammocks, beaches, pools, hotel rooms, and airplanes. Of course, that makes the book even more beautiful to me.

The main character of *Life of Pi*, Pi, got his name from Mamaji, an eccentric family friend and mentor with a talent for swimming. There is a charming story about this friend's birth and his reluctance to breathe air for the first time upon delivery. He was so fond of breathing water, clearly born to be a fish, that the doctor actually had to swing him around by his feet to make him expel the water and take his first breath. This did him a great favor because all the flesh and blood went right to his upper body giving him a perfect swimmer's body. While studying in France, Mamaji swam in every pool he could find until he found a pool that even "the gods would delight to swim in." The beauty of this pool left him amazed and speechless. The pool's name was Piscine Molitor. So, the main character of *Life of Pi* was named Piscine Molitor by a family friend with a penchant for swimming because a pool was so beautiful that it took his breath. That's quite a namesake!

However, there was a problem with this name. When you say Piscine three times fast it sounds a lot like "Pissing" to school-aged children which was of course social suicide in junior high. On the first day of school when the teacher called Piscine's name for roll, he, in an act of self-preservation and bravery leapt to his feet, dashed to the board, and wrote out his full name for everyone to see. He underlined the first two letters of his first name, explained that he was to be called Pi, and if anyone was confused, he drew the symbol for Pi and wrote out that irrationally long, irrational number. Just like that he became Pi. He did this in every class he had that day because "repetition is important in the training of minds."

Not only did Piscine become Pi, but his classmates were so respectful of the daring act that led to this simplification that they too reduced their names to symbols and called themselves just one Greek letter instead of their full, beautiful names.

What was once an outrageous, beautiful, layered, and miraculous story was now a mathematical, elusive, and irrational number, a number by which scientists try to explain the universe and one which our protagonist sought refuge.

Just like that.

Because it was easier. Less messy. Not nearly as complicated. More comfortable.

In much bigger and more beautiful ways than the main character's name, *this* is the theme of *Life of Pi*.

Life of Pi is a story about story. A deep, rich, complicated story and a man's desire to rein it all in to one tidy box, and skipping over the glorious details, forsaking the outrageous, and, consequently, living in small, predictable, gray, orderly compartments that while well-organized, are contrived and lack anything organic or Godly.

Life of Pi is a story about how our desire for truth robs us of it when we hold on to it with white knuckles in efforts to manufacture and then control it. We work miracles into stories that make sense when miracles by definition don't make sense. Ultimately, we insist, and change the truth altogether, so that we may stroll the halls of our life a little more comfortably.

We change the truth to suit ourselves.

Life of Pi celebrates that God is outrageous and that doesn't make Him any less true.

Truth is something that we can either acknowledge and celebrate or control and miss.

The book is glorious.

In the church, there is a quest for truth and everyone seems to think that they have cornered the market on exactly what that is. As churches and denominations, we stand proudly on our corners and yell out our details and skip over mystery and majesty and story and people and end up just clanging away, all the while missing the truth that we so eagerly chase. I know so many in the church who have a love of truth without having a love of *people*. Or if they do have a love of people, it is only the people who fit nicely into the constructed compartments of truth, truth that has already been determined, truth that is no longer being revealed.

Life of Pi so cleverly calls that shameful without actually calling it shameful at all. The book's message is completely left up to the reader, and rightly so, because God happens to be a real stickler on free will.

Life of Pi gives us the choice to believe that the truth is messy and layered and inconvenient and completely unbelievable. We have the option to believe the unbelievable, cope with the messy truth, and honor each other's stories and how we find God in them. Martel, I believe, yearns for us to experience this world just as it is, remarkable.

But instead...

Our relationships stay nice and neat. Just look.

Our morality is easy to measure. Just look.

Our devotion to God is evidenced. Just look.

Our faith-life is about what can be *seen* because tidy compartments are external. Our faith-lives are all about what is happening on the outside, the orderly outside.

But Jesus has something to say about this.

The Pharisees were experts at sin management and how they looked outwardly, and there may not have been a group of people with whom Jesus was more frustrated. In no uncertain terms, He let them know that their efforts were put in the wrong place, and He does it with fantastic imagery.

It turns out that a gnat was the smallest unclean animal in Palestine and the Pharisees would actually strain their liquids to make sure that they did not accidentally ingest an unclean animal (Lev 11:23). Jesus uses this practice and compares it to the largest unclean animal in Palestine, the camel (Lev 11:26), to let them know that while they focus on the minutia of the law they are missing much weightier issues. Straining gnats and swallowing camels—this is great stuff. Jesus was a clever guy.

He goes on to admonish the Pharisees for cleaning only the outside of the cup when on the inside it was littered with self-indulgence. It obviously doesn't make any sense only to focus on the outside of a dirty dish. Everyone would agree that an outwardly gleaming coffee mug inwardly lined with mold is useless, so Jesus harped on His point of the futility of external piety without addressing the darkness within.

This is just really great stuff.

He rebuked them to clean the inside of the cup first so that the outside might be clean also, and His rebuke wasn't gentle.

"Woe to you, scribes and Pharisees, hypocrites! For you tithe mint and dill and cumin, and have neglected the weightier provisions of the law: justice and mercy and faithfulness; but these are the things you should have done without neglecting the others. You blind guides, who strain out a gnat and swallow a camel! Woe to you, scribes and Pharisees, hypocrites! For you clean the outside of the cup and of the dish, but inside they are full of robbery and self-indulgence. You blind Pharisee, first clean the inside of the cup and of the dish, so that the outside of it may become clean also. Woe to you, scribes and Pharisees, hypocrites! For you are like whitewashed tombs which on the outside appear beautiful, but inside they are full of dead men's bones and all uncleanness. So you, too, outwardly appear righteous to men, but inwardly you are full of hypocrisy and lawlessness." (Matthew 23:23-28)

Jesus illustrates that it is the purity of our heart that matters most. His message tells us that holiness isn't skin deep or easily measured. And He meant it!

Clean the inside and the outside will be clean also.

That's what He said.

* * *

The greatest book that I have ever read about seeing holiness the way Jesus sees it is *Inside Out* by Dr. Larry Crabb. With simple language to describe profound thoughts, Dr. Crabb outlines in great detail the paths to freedom and personal transformation paved with truth telling. My copy is completely fluorescent yellow because every sentence is worth highlighting. I squint as I look through it again and again.

In his work that helps his readers and clients experience true transformation, Dr. Crabb starts with an inside look. There is a crucial first step to holiness and it is acknowledging something for exactly what it is, not what we wish that it were. It's acknowledging our name, however inconvenient it may be, and dealing with it without pretending that it isn't so.

I know that I am called to a holy life, but I have noticed that when it comes to trying to actually attain one, I have tendencies to be pretty unambitious. I choose some completely manageable bad habit like cussing and extricate some reprehensible word out of my sullied vocabulary and then give myself a hearty pat on the back for avoiding it ... for approximately two weeks or until the next kid gets gum in their hair or lets a popsicle melt in my bed. When it comes to holiness, I have often found that, for me, it is about lazy low hoops, uncomplicated behaviors, and getting rid of things I won't altogether miss that much. And in trying not to really miss anything, I miss Jesus' point entirely.

Cleaning up my language, refusing to gossip, eating only when I am hungry-- these things, they don't really dive into the heart of the matter, do they? They are a symptom. A completely manageable symptom. Something I can easily accomplish. *On my own.* Just a little bit of honesty and discipline are all that are really needed. Shipshape. Nice and tidy. I've got this.

But, I am convinced that Jesus isn't all that interested in symptoms that we have complete control over. Jesus really isn't all that interested in what holiness *looks* like or our attempts at trying to experience it from the outside in. Jesus isn't interested in the ways that we can clean up all on our own.

He made that abundantly clear in The Sermon on the Mount where He didn't just ask if anyone had murdered anyone but took it a step further asking if anyone had ever hated. Those two actions, He considered them the same thing. In this message of His, adultery wasn't just an action. It could be as simple as a wandering eye. Holiness, He has told us, is a matter of our hearts, our wills, our minds and our motives. The inside. The messy, filthy inside.

So what Jesus is interested in, deeply passionate about truth be told, are the complicated things inside of us that we have absolutely no control over whatsoever. The things that plague and confuse and shame us. Holiness isn't about what we can manage ourselves. Holiness is about an inside look, the complexities we find there, knowing with certainty that we cannot go it alone, and inviting God's necessary power into our lives for true transformation that we can only manage through His very own holiness. Our own outside efforts become quite silly in comparison to what God can do if given free reign inside our contaminated cup.

Messy relationships, our revealed hearts, truthful looks inside might seem unbearable, just like walking those halls as "Pissing" rather than "Pi", but true change comes from telling the truth and relying on God's power to help us change it. We can spend our whole lives taking care of gnats all by ourselves, or we can acknowledge how needy we are when it comes to camels and experience God's power. Holiness.

There is something very attractive about straining gnats and appearing holy without ever having to really let anything go. It is easy to feel good about not missing a week of Bible study, all the while hating your roommate for the boyfriend that she seems to have found so effortlessly when you can't even get asked out on a date. It is easy to feel good about donating your time to the church nursery, all the while never addressing the rage you have for your mother that is so intense that it keeps you up at night. It is easy to feel good about the new devotional you picked up, all the while never addressing the hatred you feel for your own body. It is easy to feel good about the verses you have memorized, all the while never addressing the resentment you have for your sister that has you angry about her good fortunes, and celebrating her misfortunes deep in your heart. The grudge you hold, the shame you feel, the anxiety you experience—the camels are where our pursuit of holiness starts.

True holiness is certainly about continued obedience, but joining the choir is simply not going to take care of what is really going on inside of us. While jumping through more hoops might be easier than facing inner darkness, it is an inside look that will change us from the inside out, and that is what leads us to true holiness.

But how can we do that when we won't allow discomfort?! How many times do we post our position or problem or prize on social media looking for the inevitable applause we will get there, instead of sitting with our position or problem or prize and letting God be near? How many times do we come home from a long day feeling anxious about a still-hovering to-do list and turn to the refrigerator, even though we are not hungry, instead of letting God be near? How often do we get twisted up inside over a painful interaction with a friend and take our twisted emotions to another friend to receive an "I know" instead of letting God be near? We so often take our discomfort elsewhere. We dig shallow wells trying to take care of ourselves instead of turning to the Living Water and considering that God just might want to walk that long hall with us. There might be something beautiful in the process.

To Pi, walking the halls as Piscine was insanity. He would die! But isn't that what we are after in our pursuit of holiness, in our search for intimacy with God?

Doesn't our holiness depend on dying to ourselves, our willingness to fade away? Pi desperately wanted change, but was terrified to die. He couldn't accept that the answer would never be found in a shipshape existence.

It seems as though we can't acknowledge that struggle might actually be part of the plan and *for our benefit*. These things with which we busy ourselves are oftentimes designed to bring relief when relief might not have been what was intended. Our names were given to us on purpose, quite intentionally. And we might find something beautiful in that hall as we walk proudly with our name unchanged, just as it was given.

He wants us to do more than clean the outside of the cup.

Personal transformation, the transformation that God wants for us, is internal to external. It is a transformation of our hearts and our minds and our souls that *then* begins to express itself in our actions. We have it backwards. We tend to think that all of our order and activity will take care of the things that plague us. Jesus told us plain as day that is not true. Holiness is a matter of the heart.

* * *

In college, I was learning to become a special education teacher and felt most pulled by the classrooms that were the most interesting to me. And the most interesting classrooms to me were the ones where kids were throwing chairs and desks, not just spitballs. I liked behavior units.

I was placed as a student teacher in a 9th grade behavior unit.

I have stories from this time in my life that no one believes. I broke up fights. I called parents who never answered. I called probation officers instead. I called the cops. I chased kids. I ducked flying objects. I patted them down for weapons. I diagnosed bad drug experiences, and sent many kids to the nurse terrified. I learned about a completely different way of life. Some of their mothers were prostitutes. Some of them didn't have electricity. Most of them were raised, very literally, by their street. The street that their house or apartment complex was on was responsible for their well-being. I was called every name under the sun. I have found kids in these types of classrooms to be terribly creative. Poetic even. I decided to take advantage of the creativity in the room and taught a poetry unit that they actually loved. I played Tupac and Wyclef Jean. The same creativity that made them excellent insult hurlers also made them beautiful writers. It surprised us both. And that's always the best teaching moment—when success surprises you both.

My time teaching in the behavior unit led me to want to do prison ministry. I signed up through my sorority and was to be randomly placed with a female detainee. I felt like a pro because of my time in the high school behavior unit. Meh, what's a little prison?

When I got to the maximum security State Home and asked for Monica, the guards looked at each other sideways and laughed.

"What?" I demanded. "*What*?!"

They wouldn't answer me. They just chuckled some more and said, "Good luck. That's all."

Good luck?! That's something you say before someone takes a test, or runs a race, or eats your chili. That is not something you say to someone about to meet their mentee.

I immediately started looking for exits. Not to bolt right then and there but in case I saw a shank, I needed to be prepared. Wait, was that what it was called? Shank didn't sound right all of a sudden. Dang it. I should at least know the word to detract from my naïveté. I, all of a sudden, felt so completely in over my head. Here I thought I could just smile, buy a few things out of the vending machines, bring up Tupac and Wyclef, smoothly transition to Jesus, and we would be besties. Dang it. I hate when I am so stupid stupid stupid.

I was still deciding if it was called a shank or something else when Monica walked in.

She looked relatively harmless. I mean not like me harmless, but you know, normal. She smiled. She called me "Miss." I decided to pounce on this small gesture of kindness and tell her not to ever call me Miss again because she and I were friends. And then I one-upped her and invited her to the vending machine with me and we bought one of everything.

And that did it. We were besties. Monica really liked Funyuns.

When Seth and I first started dating, he asked me what I was most proud of. I answered by talking about Monica. In a way, winning Monica took every skill that I had because the guards were right—she was difficult, she threw desks, she had seen things I couldn't imagine. We were from different worlds. Bridging that gap was a real accomplishment, for us both, and I'm certain she worked as hard as I did to meet me somewhere.

One day, several months into our relationship, there was a lull in our conversation. It was a beautiful Texas spring day and we were sitting beside the window in that sterile visiting room. I had just bought something from the vending machine and as she looked at the birds doing bird things in the trees, she sheepishly said this phrase: "I cut for you." I could tell it was difficult for her to say so I didn't make her say it again, but I didn't know what she meant. I cut for you? She looked at me and smiled kind of expectantly and I didn't know how to respond but I could clearly see that I should.

While my mind raced trying to make sense of the phrase she had just mumbled, I hesitantly said, "Thank you?." Poor Monica could read this middle class sorority girl's confusion so she clarified, "You know. Like, I cut for you."

Still searching I said, "Monica, do you mean that we are well cut out for each other? Do you mean we are a good fit?" Exasperated and laughing at me she said, "No man!!!! I *cut* for you!! Like, in the neck! I cut a ho in the neck for you!"

All at once, I was a couple of emotions, but I was all of them intensely. I was intensely appalled—she just said she would kill someone for me. In all of the ways that I had heard "I love you" in my life, this was certainly a new one. I was intensely sorry for the person who could potentially get cut, but hey, don't mess with me. But mostly I was intensely flattered. I fell more in love with Monica that day.

Then, the next visit, this happened.

I showed up like normal. Bought her favorite snacks like normal. We chitchatted mostly like normal but I could tell something was on her mind. I asked her if she was OK, was something going on? She took a deep breath. Silence. Another deep breath and then she said, "I ain't told you e'rything. You don't know e'rything about why I'm here. I only told you parts I like. After last time you was here, I thought something. I cut for you. But if I don't know that you cut for me too then it ain't right. Feels like I put it in the wrong place. And I know you think you cut for me too because you sit here and we watch the birds, but what if what I keep from you is the only reason you still here? It ain't right. You cut for me because you think you know me. But maybe you don't. I guess it's time you know me. All a me. Before it don't matter, but now maybe it do."

I was stunned.

All I wanted to do was protect her vulnerability in that moment. She was struggling. She was uncomfortable. And all I wanted to do was to make it stop. So I said, "Monica, you don't have to do this. I don't want to know. There is not one thing that you could say that would make me change my mind about you. So, forget it and know that I love you anyway. You just don't have to do this for me. I think—"

"Damn woman! Ain't you just hear a word I said? It ain't for *you*. I need you to know. You right I don't wanna say it, but don't you see I have to? You talk good, but sometimes you don't listen so good."

"Oh. Yes. Right." Stunned again. I decided to finally shut up and let Monica do what Monica needed to do.

I would never want to reduce Monica to what she did. It was awful. She told me every bit of it. The story that she told me before was impersonal, removed, violent, she shared the responsibility. In this new story, she was the only perpetrator. It was very personal. She told me details that she definitely could have left out. Her crime landed her in a juvenile detention center, but it was a terrible fight in that juvenile detention center that put her in a maximum security State Home.

She looked me in the eye the whole time she spoke. It was I who looked away. And it wasn't because I was appalled by what I heard. It was certainly surprising, but my shame was something different. I couldn't believe her bravery. I couldn't believe her willingness to unpack this mess before me. With whom was I willing to sit down and give away my ugliest parts when they hadn't even asked for them? I couldn't think of anyone.

The State Home where Monica was detained worked on a point system. Detainees could "earn" their way out with levels of accomplishment that demonstrated good behavior and showed responsibility. External. Detainees had to keep their rooms tidy and turn in their homework and pass their classes and get along well with others. Monica wasn't consistently good at many of those. She would do well for a while and then lose her temper. She would work off of will power for a while and then fall apart with her schoolwork. She was never able to work the system. She could never get her outsides in order. But her insides? I realized I had a lot to learn. I worked the system just fine, but at that point in my life, I could never have done what she did. That would have been far too complicated, far too uncomfortable.

Was it her upbringing that made her so fearless? How she grew up, was that what made her so unafraid of the discomfort that she instinctively knew was for her own good? Could that ransacked mess of a childhood actually be her blessing? And could the protection of my cushy, nurturing, sparkly environments be the barrier to more important blessings than those could ever offer? I was bowled over that day by her bravery.

I love Monica. At age twenty-one, the State Home had to release her but she had nowhere to go. Her family was in San Antonio and couldn't come get her. So I did. She stayed with me for a couple of weeks but that was no solution. I eventually ended up taking her back to her family. We met at a train station. And I never saw Monica again. Her family moved a lot and she didn't have a phone so I had no way to tell her that I was moving. And that was it.

I have thought of her one million times since. I have prayed for her heartily and hoped she wasn't in trouble or hungry or scared or lonely. I have prayed for the continued purity of her heart. I love Monica.

* * *

Our holiness is not connected to just our outsides. Christ wants us to climb down into the inside of our cup and do something about the filth. He is trying to direct us into the dark places of our soul. He wants us to find Him there. He wants us to experience His presence where we feel the most ugly. And maybe then that experience begins to express itself in our actions.

True holiness does not require that we pretend that things are anything other than what they are. Christ wants us to face reality as it is—the fear, resentment, jealousy, harsh judgments, rage, and the ugly motives that we work to keep out of sight—He wants us to invite Him there so that we can emerge as changed people more aware of His love. Inside first, outside because.

I think about Monica and the beauty that existed between us, the beauty for which she was responsible. I certainly wouldn't calculate starting a friendship that way. I think sharing a nice cup of coffee while discussing a common interest would be my first plan. But maybe chai lattes and yoga are a lot like those compartments we've been talking about. Maybe macchiatos and knitting are pretty similar to that irrational number.

Maybe complicated and vulnerable is a lot like that messy, layered, outrageous story. Maybe uncomfortable and unplanned is similar to that fantastic and downright unbelievable tale about how a boy got his name. I'm learning that honesty has some great surprises up her sleeve. And if applied everywhere, how blessed I might be.

"Create in me a clean heart, O God, And renew a steadfast spirit within me." (Psalm 51:10)

TO CONSIDER:

1. In what ways do you seek to remain comfortable? Do any of these ways sacrifice what God may be calling you to do? Do any of them sacrifice holiness?

2. Is truth something that you hold open-handed or clutch tightly? What is the right balance?

3. Is the outside of your cup clean while the inside is messy? Or is your inside clean and the outside a mess? Or are both a little dirty? Describe your cup.

4. How have you not let God be near?

TO PRACTICE:

Think about your darkest struggle. Put words to it in a prayer journal. When the time is right share your thoughts with a trusted friend.

TO LISTEN:

1. "Altar of Love" by Downhere

2. "Here's My Heart" by David Crowder

CHAPTER 9:

Lifted Kiwis & Little Climbs

"Start by doing what's necessary; then do what's possible; and suddenly you are doing the impossible."
—ST. FRANCIS OF ASSISI

W hen I start my day off right, it begins with the prayer, "Here I am. Send me."

I frequently have grand notions of waking up before the kids, starting the coffee, waiting for it to finish brewing while I find my place in my Bible, and sitting down at the breakfast table to... you know... have a moment. It's like a Folgers commercial—all the peace that I imagine would happen in those twenty minutes.

While it's a good idea, it never quite comes to fruition.

In practice, starting my day off "right" looks like three little heads at the edge of my side of the bed, with the littlest, chubbiest hands on my cheeks turning my face towards his so that we can have eye contact when he says, "Mommy! Lucky Chawms! My belly needs mawshmallows." Because I've been up with the baby throughout the night, my husband gets up to feed them marshmallows while I lie in bed and wonder when we will ever sleep again.

Marshmallows. Maybe the trick is marshmallows, not Folgers. It seems to be working for my children. It's worth a shot so I swing out of bed and occasionally, if I remember, pine for my commercial setting of a quiet time, modify the heck out of it, and simply repeat after Isaiah, saying, "Here I am. Send me" (Isaiah 6:8), as I stumble to the pantry for my own dose of marshmallows. When it comes to morning quiet times, that's usually the best that I get.

As modified as it is, it is still *something*. In fact, since the beginning of my commitment to this short prayer, however foggy it is recited, I have found myself in some dynamic situations, and I don't believe in coincidences anymore.

That prayer has been a catalyst.

I just know it.

It might be tempting to think that my prayer has led God to transform my circumstances, but I know that He really has simply transformed *me*. Rather than God finally allowing me opportunities to do some good work, my eyes have just been opened to the opportunity for good work all around me, every day.

Isn't that more likely?

If it's not in the Nicene Creed, I try not to make grand, certain statements about God, things I know *for sure*. This mindset allows me to stay light on my feet, open to the Spirit, willing to learn, teachable in general, and it also allows me to be a safe place to talk and process thoughts with brothers and sisters. I think this mindset helps me with the poverty of spirit that I am called to have; it helps me maintain a stance of utter dependence before God.

While it is important to have enough humility to be able to say *I know that I do not have everything right*, I do know that I have this right: God has used my prayer to make me more aware of the work that He has for me. "Here I am. Send me." By saying this each day, I walk among His people differently.

I have been changed.

My eyes have been opened.

I know it.

For sure.

Sadly, I have to admit that what I meant when I started praying the "Here I am. Send me," prayer, was that I hoped God would choose me to be a major player in His most challenging battles. I wanted Him to find me worthy of talking people off of ledges. I envisioned myself praying a thousand Sinners' Prayers in coffee shops, on campuses, on my couch, at death's door. I wanted to swoop in and save the day. I wanted to fight addiction, selfishness, apathy, and greed all in His name and all for His glory. A cape! I wanted a cape! *Here I am! Send me!*

I jest.

But only a little.

It is true that I said my prayer like an anxious kindergartner might, waving her hand around with a "Pick me! Pick me!" mantra. My only work really being to just keep flailing, waiting to be called on, hoping with all hope to be noticed. I hoped my prayer was a catalyst to being chosen so that I might then be used mightily for dramatic conversions.

But that is not what has come to pass.

Instead, what I have found is that my prayer is a reminder that I have already been chosen and that I am to be used finely for loving interactions.

* * *

I had an epiphany at the grocery store that made me realize something very embarrassing. In the middle of the produce section at our local H-E-B grocery store, I learned that my initial motivator in praying the prayer was to be *influential*. I hate to admit it, but I wanted to be a little miniature God walking around my community granting peace and salvation and wellbeing. It's a difficult confession. I had to shut my eyes while I typed it.

Influence? Is that what we're called to?

No, I don't think so. Influence might be a beautiful byproduct, but first and foremost, we are called to surrender our lives to Christ.

We are called to be loving.

Desiring influence is the proverbial cart before the horse.

Hoping for influence without full submission has very little to do with God and a whole lot to do with ego.

After my grocery store epiphany, I got my horses and carts in the right order. "Here I am. Send me," has now taken on a new meaning, despite my initial desires for grandeur.

It was a Friday morning and I had all four kids at H-E-B.

Wait, I just made that sound simple, didn't I?

Let me rephrase that. I had entered an Olympic event called Roll-A-Cart-Full-Of-Demanding-Fighting-Needy-Children-Around-A-Store-Filled-With-Things-They-Want-And-Things-You-Need (No, of course those are not the same things) -And-See-If-You-Can-Get-Out-Unscathed-With-All-Of-The-Appropriate-Materials-And-None-Of-The-Crap-And-All-Of-Your-Children. Good luck!

On this day in particular, I was in the produce section. My kids were spilling out of the grocery cart. My third child had his Spiderman tennis shoe planted right in the middle of the loaf of bread (when will I learn to get the bread last?), while my oldest, intent on helping, sent a pyramid of apples tumbling to the ground. As I scolded everyone through clenched teeth, I saw a friend with her kids who were doing about the same things that mine were, minus the rolling apples. We looked at each other, relieved to be in the same boat. She helped me pick up the apples. When we finished, we chatted for a bit, and as we were talking, I noticed that her attention was divided. Her eyes kept being pulled away. I followed her gaze and saw that she was looking at a young woman wearing a hijab who was inspecting a kiwi. I saw nothing unusual about the young woman and couldn't help but wonder why my friend was checking out of our conversation to watch this girl.

Finally, as though she couldn't restrain herself anymore, she blurted out, "I'm so sorry but can you hold on a second?"

"Sure," I started to say, but before I even had time to get the word out, she was walking towards this young woman. I watched from about fifteen feet away wondering if she already knew this person and needed to say hello. The next few seconds let me know that they did not know each other.

My friend walked up gently. She extended her hand. She smiled. She was doing most of the talking. The young woman looked at her feet, only occasionally glancing up to smile. She was still holding the kiwi. My friend started to gesture towards it. She appeared to be rambling on while the young woman smiled more and more, looking up and meeting her eyes with more frequency.

I was still wondering why my friend interrupted our conversation and trusted me with her kids when my own were sending produce rolling, when all of a sudden, I saw her take the kiwi from the young woman, get her car keys out of her purse, use one to cut the fruit open, and proudly hold it up dripping while she and this stranger laughed together.

The young woman was shocked. Her mouth open in a smile. She looked around to see who was watching, if they might get in trouble. My friend, unconcerned with all of that, pointed out the vibrant color of the fruit. There was more talking, and laughing, some sticky handshaking, and then my friend headed back our way. She grabbed a plastic bag off the roller on her way and wrapped the kiwi in it. I just looked at her waiting for an explanation. She put her keys back in her purse along with the kiwi and said matter-of-factly, "That's Sabina. She's a student. She had never seen a kiwi before."

Right.

She had never seen a kiwi before. (They are weird little fruits, aren't they?) I stood there staring at my friend bewildered... amazed... inspired.

We were in the grocery store with our children.

We were in a conversation.

There were rolling apples and whining children and smashed loaves of bread.

There was an international student looking at a kiwi with a perplexed facial expression, practically halfway across the produce section.

And my friend had the selflessness in the midst of all of that to realize that this person was far away from home? That this person was in a foreign land with no family to accompany her? That she had perhaps never seen a kiwi and had no clue what it was? My friend had the selflessness to consider that the young woman's existence was possibly a lonely and confusing one?

My friend's selflessness stunned me. But, it wasn't just her selflessness that stunned me. It was her *awareness*.

It was as though she were *looking* for an opportunity to love someone.

Right.

Well.

How about that.

"Here I am. Send me."

We are called to love.

And that was my epiphany. We are called to love. How many different ways had I heard it before?

What she did, it wasn't a big deal. She introduced herself to a stranger and stole a kiwi. (She could have paid for it, I don't know.) It took six minutes of her time. She loved her neighbor as though it wasn't a metaphor. She actually acted loving towards her neighbor. Seeing her own "Here I am. Send me," in action begged the question: How much time do I waste frantically waving my hand around, waiting to be chosen for a God-sized mountain, only to miss the people-sized mountains all around me every minute of every day?

What she did, it wasn't a big deal. But it was to me. And it probably was to Sabina.

I had a revelation that day. God has done the Big Thing. Jesus came. Jesus died. Jesus rose.

The big work?

It is finished.

So now? For me? Well, I just get to live the best way that I can. I just get to do the things that please Him. I am not here to be a miniature God moving mountains every day in a cape. I am here to live my life in gratitude of grace and serve Him well and also those around me. He made it that simple for me.

Yes, I long for my life to have meaning. I long to live a life that matters. I long to be influential. But I learned that my impacting life is not dependent upon ambitious or thrilling mountains. My impacting life is using the strengths He gave me to love those around me. Influence might be a byproduct of loving well, but it is nothing to focus on. Love is.

There are mountains everywhere. A million times a day. Little mountains to climb with the love that He gave first, motivating my steps whether they be exciting or mundane, challenging or effortless.

The goal of a disciple of Jesus is not to walk around looking for God-sized mountains to move. The goal of a disciple of Jesus is to walk around looking for His people to love a million times every day, on a minute-by-minute basis. The goal is to go about our lives walking in His will, looking for people-sized mountains around every corner, in every aisle.

And isn't that a better measuring stick of our faith? Not the size of our mountain but how we treat those climbing next to us? Isn't the true indicator of our love for Him how we love others? Isn't that what obedience looks like? Aren't the details of my love for Him found in how I respond to a friend who boasts, a relative who is passive-aggressive, an acquaintance who is aggressive-aggressive, a colleague who is a know-it-all, a barista who is grumpy? How I handle being cut off in traffic, or how I interact with the person asking for my spare change, or how I look for lonely people in the places I frequent? Do not the daily interactions with those around me define me more?

What if that was what defined my life? How diligently I pursued love regarding whatever or whomever it was that He put before me that day? What if my faith wasn't about grandstanding or gaining attention or ascending treacherous mountains? What if my faith were truly about my ever-evolving relationship with Him? What if it were about service and love, and as many mountains as there are neighbors? Nothing more, nothing less.

* * *

I work closely with college seniors and the idea of that one big mountain can be debilitating. These girls, with the rest of their lives ahead of them and seemingly resting on the one decision they make that semester— the one, big, God-sized mountain—it paralyzes them. They are afraid of making a wrong decision. They are afraid of climbing the wrong mountain. They question their own judgment. They measure their steps. They stare at the peak of the mountain they desire to conquer and become overwhelmed by fear and insecurity. Do they really have what it takes? A panicky stagnation sets in.

After our Bible Study, a sweetheart college girl asked to stay and talk to me afterwards. The crowd dissipated and it was just she and I over an empty plate of cookie crumbs. She fumbled for words, before just blurting out, "There's no other way to put it, but God just didn't make me special. And I'm pretty upset with Him about it. I don't have any talents. I don't have any gifts. Nothing makes me stand out. I'm average. I am so tired of being average."

As I was listening to her, I conjured up the emotions she described. I knew exactly the feelings that she outlined. My heart remembered and went out to her. In fact, I remembered so vividly that I forgot I was there to be a *mentor* instead of a *friendtor*. I nodded with her. I empathized and got lost in her feelings before remembering that I was supposed to be there offering wisdom.

Quite frequently, these precious girls will ask me something and I will have a "DUH!" moment, realizing I am expected to have an answer. When these moments happen, I do the only thing I can do and pray, "Come,

Holy Spirit." Not once have I been left stammering on my own. Not once.

When I snapped out of the familiar feelings of mediocrity and prayed for the Spirit to come, I found myself re-centered and able to speak. This came out:

I know what you mean. I have had that exact feeling. You described it so well and I know it so well that for a moment I was actually lost in remembering how bland it feels. And, you know what? I don't feel that way anymore. And now that you have made me analyze it, I know why. You are why I don't feel that way anymore. This moment. These conversations. I am not average. I am used by the Holy Spirit to do beautiful work that glorifies His name.

Sweetheart, God is tired of you feeling average, too. He certainly didn't make you that way. That is a lie that you have believed.

I think it's possible that you're spending too much time looking for a grandiose way to make an impact. And that's not how impact works. Enough with the impact. I guarantee there was someone around you today who needed something you could give. Who was it? Quit looking to the top of the mountain. Look beside you. Look around! But do it. Now. Quit analyzing it and just do it.

Loving is what is going to make you feel special. When you serve using your gifts, you will recognize

195

God's great call for you and there just isn't a better feeling than being used by Him. There's just nothing average about it.

* * *

In Luke 16, Jesus tells a mystifying little parable about a man who mismanaged his master's money, got caught, and was promptly fired. In hopes of covering his tail, this man smudged some numbers thereby cheating his boss out of money, and, for showing such shrewdness, ended up being praised by the very boss that he had cheated! You can't make this stuff up:

"Now He was also saying to the disciples, 'There was a rich man who had a manager, and this manager was reported to him as squandering his possessions. And he called him and said to him, "What is this I hear about you? Give an accounting of your management, for you can no longer be manager."'" (Luke 16:1-2)

Right after being fired, the man calls in his boss's debtors and starts slashing their debts. In order to be welcomed into their homes, since now he is jobless and could probably use a few friends, he says, "You! What do you owe?! 900 gallons? Make it 450!" When his boss hears of this, he commends "the unrighteous manager because he had acted shrewdly; for the sons of this age are more shrewd in relation to their own kind than the sons of light. And I say to you, make friends for yourselves by means of the wealth of unrighteousness, so that when it fails, they will receive you into the eternal dwellings." (Luke 16:8-9)

This is baffling, is it not? The manager of the rich man's money, upon realizing that he is about to become jobless and homeless, hatches a devious plan to take care of himself because he is not willing to do manual labor and is too proud to beg.

And he is commended?

This guy—he was sneaky, lazy, and cunning. Let's face it, he was a hustler! I have to admit that this parable was a head-scratcher for me. Was Jesus really commending dishonesty?

I have read many different explanations of this parable of the Rich Man and the Shrewd Manager. I can't wait to sit at His feet one day and know what it all means *for sure*. But I'll tell you that the day after I watched my friend slice open an unpurchased kiwi in order to make a stranger laugh and feel welcome in her presence, the message that came to me from this parable was about shrewdness. My friend was shrewd. *With her love*.

Her gifts of warmth and gregariousness that had been given to her by our Lord, she used them shrewdly. The "money" that the master trusted her with, she poured it out lavishly. She was generous with what she had at her disposal. She was generous with her Master's gifts that he trusted her with, and she used them to win favor. She was shrewd with a kingdom currency.

Shrewdness is about *response*. Response is about *action*. And action isn't sitting around flailing my hand in the air waiting to be called on. I've already been called on! The waiting, the flailing, the analysis, the paralysis, the desire for grandiosity—they keep me from my climb.

What would it look like if I channeled my survival instincts, covering my own behind, to my spiritual life?

May that be the lesson?

What if I understood with my heart that all the riches that I manage are only in my possession because of the Master? What if I understood that my gifts didn't belong to me and weren't necessarily for my benefit? What if I finally got that they were actually given to me for the benefit of others? My gifts are on purpose and for someone else! Could it really be true?

While I sat there waving my hand in the air, and my precious college girl stood still staring up a hill, my friend in the grocery store had already loved more people than we had even noticed were there. While we sat there hoping for influence, there she was being influential, unconcerned with the size of her mountain and concerned only with dispensing her gifts. Shrewdly.

In the days, weeks and years that have followed that Friday morning in the H-E-B grocery store, my morning prayer has transformed a bit. It is still mumbled groggily over marshmallows, but these days it is less about me, less about mountains, less about waiting, and it is more about my neighbor, more about my response, more about my shrewdness. "Here I am. Send me," is no longer a grand appeal to be led to the foot of an impressive mountain, frantically waving my hand while I wait. There is no need to wait. The mountains are everywhere with all of our names on them, in need of each other's gifts.

"As each one has received a special gift, employ it in serving one another as good stewards of the manifold grace of God." (1 Peter 4:10)

TO CONSIDER:

1. Do you waste any time waiting to feel chosen?
2. How do you define success in your life? Which accomplishments matter the most to you?
3. How might focusing on Little Love instead of God-sized impact affect your day to day?
4. What mountain are you standing daunted at the foot of? What do you need to get moving? How might you be shrewd?

TO PRACTICE:

Consider your gifts. Choose your favorite one about yourself. Use it to do one act of kindness per week for one month.

TO LISTEN:

1. "Sweet Comfort" by Sandra McCracken
2. "Build Your Kingdom Here" by Rend Collective

AFTERWORD:

One More Thing...

*"If Jesus gives us a task or assigns us to a difficult
season, every ounce of our experience is meant for
our instruction and completion if only we'll let
Him finish the work. I fear, however, that we
are so attention-deficit that we settle for bearable
when beauty is just around the corner."*
—BETH MOORE

In the Gospel of Luke, we are told of a story where
Jesus was preaching on the edge of the sea. Many people
pressed in to listen. Running out of room, Jesus decided
to teach from an empty boat so that more people could
see and hear. After finishing His teaching, Jesus told
Simon to get in his boat and go fish where the sea was

deepest. There, Jesus assured Simon, many fish would be caught.

Simon responded respectfully, but basically told Jesus in so many words (fine, it's my own rendition), *Well, I just did that. All night actually. And it didn't produce much. But since you have hundreds of people here to listen to you and all, maybe I should listen to you, too, so okay, I'll do that... if you say so.*

All of a sudden, there were so many fish that the nets were breaking and he needed backup. Simon saw this and fell to his knees. He said he wasn't good enough to be around this man. But Jesus told him not to be afraid and assured him that now he would be fishing for men. Simon left everything behind and followed Him. (Luke 5:1-11)

What I love about this is that Simon told Jesus, this doesn't really make sense, but I'll give it a shot. I'll do it because you asked me to do it.

I'm puzzled, but okay.

Simon did as he was asked. He was obedient and faithful and his action glorified the Lord.

And the reward was plentiful, for God will not be outdone. And if not here on Earth, then in heaven. Our faithfulness is never ignored.

There is no such thing as failure if you are listening to God and giving what He asks of you a shot. That's it. That's life. That's what it is. Listening and giving it a shot.

Because aren't we all either hiding from or seeking some Godly possibility?

* * *

I love God.

I love women.

And I love to write.

In that order.

I started loving the Lord in high school. I started loving other women in college. I started loving to write when I became a mother.

I keep a blog for our family and it was there that I turned into "one who writes," or rather, because I have always written, one who *needs* to write. I think for most people who have a blog, it might be the other way around. They write, so they keep a blog. I blogged for our family, so I wrote. And as I did so, I felt a slow transition taking place over the years. Like a river tosses around a rock, smoothing out its jagged edges, showing up to write week after week seemed to be softening me.

Staring into that screen and searching my heart turned into sacred space, space that seemed to make me more *me*. Logging on and banging out the details of our family slowly turned into a necessary practice, a practice I needed to protect... from little people. Because let's face it, I can't go to the bathroom without fingers reaching for me under the door. It would have certainly been easier to deny the part of me that rested in writing, but something happened at my dentist's office that let me know that was not an option. It came about like this:

I needed a root canal.

I am terrified of the dentist.

Probably because I have never, ever gone to the dentist without them telling me I had at least three cavities, which, by the way, when you've had eight, sounds like a perfectly reasonable number. Every time I go, I brace myself for the number, and every time the hygienist smiles a part sympathetic yet judging smile and tells me that I probably just have "soft teeth." She, with her hard teeth, is trying to make me feel better and I appreciate that she cares about my feelings. Soft-toothed people are people, too.

So, I needed a root canal. I geared up for days. I had just had an unmedicated delivery and told myself that if I could turn my uterus inside out without drugs, I could handle a teeny, tiny drill. And yet, I'm now sweating as I type the word "drill." I showed up early so the receptionist could pray for me. She does that, that Tina. Especially if you come in looking like me—wild-eyed, disheveled, and talking frantically about who knows what.

They ushered me into the room with soft, slow talking and reassuring smiles, holding my hand like I wasn't just a dental patient but perhaps some other kind of patient. I lay in the chair. There was a TV on the ceiling. How about that? It was on the Food Network. I found it completely ironic that it was on a candy show, but whatever, I wasn't expecting adult entertainment and this was a definite plus.

I put in my ear buds and turned up my music as loud as it would go and watched two very nice ladies make the most beautiful caramels I had ever seen. I concentrated on not audibly humming to my music and changed the channel to Rachel Ray once the caramels had set. And then, I had this thought:

This is kind of nice. Getting a root canal is kind of nice.

Wait. What?

Well.

That's sad.

This is not ok!

There were two people four inches from my face staring into my open mouth, their fingers moving my tongue around, drilling a hole deep into my head, and yet I truly felt like I was having some *me* time. The morning was similar to time spent at a spa! It was very spa-like, actually.

This was a desperate situation. One should not need to get nerves and pulp removed in order to have a little peace and quiet. While I was thankful that my root canal was not miserable, a date with my dentist should not be *that* enjoyable. I admitted I had a situation.

So I made a decision right then and there. My blog, my writing, my space online, not my dentist's space, was going to be my calm, quiet space. My root canal was an eye opener that something had to give. I needed something just for me besides dentist appointments.

I was skeptical that such a thing truly existed while raising babies—space. I bathe with farm animals and dinosaurs floating around me. I have once hidden in a closet that they don't know about. And yet, God is mighty. He, after all, spoke light into place. Surely He could make the days a little longer, my house a little quieter, my load a little lighter so that every once in a while with some regularity, I might set aside needed time to read and write about Him so I don't need to return to my dentist's office.

And that's how it happened. That's how I came to depend on writing as a way of life for me.

* * *

I was talking to my spiritual advisor about how I felt led to writing but felt burdened by how average it all seems to come out. She said, "Allison, how does life come to you? I've never read anything you've written except for a few emails, but I can tell just by talking to you that life comes to you in words. *That* is what makes you a writer. Who cares if it's any good?!"

And with that, I have picked up my pace, and finished a book that I never thought I could write.

It's possible that I only have one book in me, but I know that I won't quit writing. And I can't quite explain that. It's just what I do. It's just who I am. It is who I have always been. *It's how life comes to me.* And I've just finally decided to quit arguing with it.

I was responsible for crafting everyone's love letters in elementary school. When one of my dearest had her baby, she asked me to explain to our friends how she brought her first born into the world. When another of my dearest was speechless after a breakup, I gave words to her heavy heart and wrote her response to his *I Think We Should Just Be Friends* letter.

I think in blog posts. I try to make my grocery lists rhyme. For better or worse, I love words. I love to write. It calms a restlessness I have never been able to put my finger squarely on. I steal moments to do it. I stay up late to try to do it well. When I daydream of a perfect day it always includes creating something written. When my husband is cranky, it is because it has been too long since he has worked out. When I am cranky, it is because it has been too long since I have written.

I write because I feel like I am supposed to. And I am not sure we can choose for ourselves that which we are supposed to do.

I feel led to writing.

Even at very inconvenient times, I feel led to it—when I'd rather sleep or watch TV or finish a book. I have crawled out of bed in the middle of the night to jot down some ideas because I have found it is then that I am the least judgmental of the timid little words that crawl out. With a baby in my arms and a toddler on my lap and cups of juice dangerously close, I have henpecked, one-handed, words that seem to want to be written. I have paused in the middle of labor, baby-producing labor, in order to tell a story that I think needs told.

Do I enjoy it? When it's done.

Does it make me happy? When I feel like God showed up.

And sometimes He really does.

Other times I feel like I force it.

But those times when I don't, when I quit trying so dang hard to sound deep, when I concentrate on getting something down rather than thinking something up, that's when words that have miraculously made their way through me and on to the page seem to matter most. If I am ever proud of anything I have written, it is because I let it shape itself. The stuff I like always seems to happen in spite of me, by accident. And that is when I celebrate, when it had nothing to do with me.

It's when He shows up that I know I am right where I am supposed to be. The words are not conjured or deliberated. They are not on command. They occasionally just... come... requiring only my partnership, not my rule.

God made me. I'm not quite sure yet why He made me this way when I wrestle with how well I am supposed to be doing this thing He has left me with. And yet, He made me. I can't tell Him anything new about me, but instead He can tell me new things about myself. He is the original Writer.

Yes. I deeply love God. But I have at times felt like I don't love God very well because I have watched other people make it seem easier. And yes, I deeply love women. But, I have at times wondered if I'm doing it wrong because it seems other people aren't struggling with relationships. And yes, I deeply love to write to express myself. But I have often thought myself silly because there are so many other people with more beautiful things to say. But what if, what if by embracing what we feel led to do, we were taught something about some of our greatest loves?

To be honest, publishing a book makes me feel incredibly sheepish. There are probably only fifteen people in the whole world who know that I have attempted this, and here it is, the Afterword. But because I have stepped out in faith, trusting that God may know something that I don't, I will lean into this feeling of foolishness instead of running away from it, and realize that life isn't all about my complex feelings.

Sometimes it can just be as simple as throwing the net or not. Perhaps my feelings shouldn't govern my every action. Perhaps.

When I talk to my husband about the anxiety that comes with the thought of people knowing that I wrote a book, I find it annoying how easy things are for him. I will ramble on for moments on end and he will smile and nod and soothe my plentiful emotions and rock in the rocking chair on our porch and think and listen and validate me. He will do all of that, but in the end, in the very end, it always comes down to only this: *What you are doing, does it glorify God, or not? If yes, then keep doing it. Keep it up. If no, then don't.*

* * *

I had this dream in relation to writing for an audience and while I found my subconscious clever, I did not find it very cryptic.

I was at a flea market. There were tons and tons of racks of really cute inexpensive clothes. I loaded up my arms and looked around for the nearest dressing room. A helpful, handsome, quiet, dark-skinned man rushed to my side and took my clothes from me and led me to a very spacious dressing room. I smiled and thanked him generously for giving me such a large room. I suspected he had shown me some favor in leading me to this room that was a little inconvenient to get to, yet very nice.

He carefully laid my clothes down on a bench beside me, but when I looked down at them to see what I would try on first, I realized that they had all turned into swimsuits. Swimsuits?! I did not want to try on swimsuits! In fact, I'd rather eat glass. But I remembered that I did actually need a swimsuit for our trip coming up in July and maybe it was just this nice man's way of taking care of me by insisting that I do something I would really rather not do.

I smiled at what a thoughtful, if not a little annoying, man he was and tried on the first one, a lovely aqua number. I surveyed how much cellulite was showing in the back and right at that moment, I heard a ding. This ding sounded a lot like an elevator ding. *That's weird*, I thought, and then I realized that my dressing room had an elevator in it and an elevator was opening into my dressing room... where I was trying on... swimsuits... of all things.

I saw two doors sliding open and about fifteen people standing there staring at me in the aqua swimsuit that was truthfully a little too small. Awesome. I stared at them. They stared at me. It was awful. I'd like to say that everyone started clapping but they didn't. I can't remember what they did. I think they went about their business. I think they barely noticed me.

See? Pretty straightforward. In one way, writing is as fun as finding fantastic bargains at a flea market and in another way, it is a lot like trying on swimsuits with an audience. But I feel led to this place very much on Purpose. It feeds my soul. And for some reason, that Kind Man apparently thinks I should wear an aqua number, cellulite and all.

So... *if you say so.*

Even if no one notices.

Of course, it's easier to stay put, to write for my family, where everyone loves me, where everyone agrees with me, but the Lord isn't interested in my comfort, He is interested in my conversion. And why are we so convinced that things that hurt like hell are bad for us anyway?

Am I worried about failure?

Am I worried about criticism?

Am I worried about going unnoticed?

Sure!

But I am certain, that if I am truly following a Godly tug that says *do it*, then those things, perhaps painful, will be for my benefit.

Failure, criticism, and vulnerability are undoubtedly going to foster humility as I give this a shot. Should any glory come from it, the hurt will keep me grounded, keep me from taking any credit for whatever gifts He may have shared using me. Humility, after all, is such a crucial part as we use our gifts correctly. There will be hurt, but it will be useful, and frankly, I am more concerned with hiding a gift over using it mistakenly, recklessly, obtusely.

* * *

Jesus tells us the consequences of hiding our gifts in His Parable of the Talents. (Matthew 25:14-30) In this story, a man was going on a journey, but before he left, he handed out talents to his slaves. He gave one five talents, another two, and the last one he gave one only, all according to their abilities. The slave who had been given five talents worked, traded, and gained five more. The slave who received two did the same, making two more. But the slave who received only one talent went and buried it.

When the master came back and the slaves reported their earnings, to the ones who doubled their talents he said, "Well done, good and faithful slave. You were faithful with a few things, I will put you in charge of many things; enter into the joy of your master." (Matthew 25:21)

But when the last slave confessed that he was afraid and buried his talent the master said, "You wicked, lazy slave, you knew that I reap where I did not sow and gather where I scattered no seed. Then you ought to have put my money in the bank, and on my arrival I would have received my money back with interest.

Therefore take away the talent from him, and give it to the one who has the ten talents." (Matthew 25: 26-28)

I can think of so many loved ones who have so clearly been given five talents. I sit around a table with thirteen of them once a week. I talk to one twice a day at least. I was raised by two of them. I am married to another. Countless acquaintances, peers, and friends who are so very talented. I am not being falsely humble when I submit that I think that I am in the camp of those who have been given two talents. I'm not a five-talent carrier.

But look, I have a point. I am not necessarily in danger of burying my one talent due to fear. I don't think I will do that. But you know what I do think that I have proclivities to do? Look around at the people with five talents, look down at the two in my hand, wish it were five, and become paralyzed, looking from side to side instead of outward and upward.

The Parable of the Talents tells me to go and risk and get out there regardless of those who are finding greater success, and regardless of those who are playing it safe.

So, I have no formal training as a writer. So what?! It's what feeds my soul!

In a field of radiant wildflowers, this book is a wispy buttercup, but precious to me and my Lord all the same.

I would rather pour myself out and hear crickets than sit around comfortably with a talent clutched in my sweaty hand.

That thing that makes you cranky when you don't do it? What is it?

Sister, is there something He wants you to do?

Do you feel a stirring in your heart to try something new?

Is there anything you want to explore but feel afraid to mess up?

Do it!

Mess up!

Give Him a chance to surprise you.

Give Him a chance to take you down a road you didn't know that you wanted to see.

Let Him comfort you when things get screwy.

Let Him encourage you when it isn't going your way.

Let Him assure you that His way is always best.

Let God be near.

Be obedient. Glorify the Lord. Faithfulness is never ignored.

"Whatever your hand finds to do, do it with all your might; for there is no activity or planning or knowledge or wisdom in Sheol where you are going." (Ecclesiasates 9:10)

To Consider:

1. How easy is it for you to answer the Lord's requests even though they may not make sense? Have you ever felt pulled to do something that didn't make sense at the time? Did it make sense later?

2. Describe a time when analysis led to paralysis and kept you from something you should have done.

3. What is it that when you do it, it makes you feel more like you? What is it, that when kept from it, makes you cranky?

4. Are you currently contemplating a change or a challenge?

To Practice:

Decide what it is that you need to make space to do in order to feel more like who God created you to be. Come up with a specific plan about how to incorporate that activity into your days and weeks.

To Listen:

1. "Hear the Sound" by All Sons and Daughters

2. "Finally Home" by Mercy Me

ACKNOWLEDGMENTS

"Thank you" sounds like a pretty silly way to express the considerable, even cumbersome, emotion that lies heavy on my chest. There are so many people that I want to squeeze until it hurts us both a little.

First, my mom and dad. It was my mom who taught me to roll words around, notice them, play with them, use them lovingly, sharply, comically, therapeutically. Anyone who has received a letter from my mom has kept it in a safe place. I have them by the dozens. And, I can hear exactly the tone of my dad's voice and see the light in his eyes when he says, "There's a book in you, girl." As an only child and the adored member of our trio I owe every confidence I have to being loved well in a house that knew no boundaries when it came to giving and nurture and selflessness and encouragement and hospitality, mixed in with a just a wee bit of the most delightful crazy. I am whole-heartedly thankful for what you gave and gave and gave and how you extended yourselves in ways that were probably uncomfortable so that I could learn life-giving lessons an easier way than you two ever did. I'm certain that I still don't know all of the ways that you have sacrificed for me. Being raised by people who would wake up in the middle of the night to smell my hair was always a difficult thing to explain to my overnight guests as a kid. "It's my parents, they just really love me."

Best friend, abbreviated to Be Fri, affectionately dubbed Beefy, and Beef for short, Kristen Werner Kelly. Ah, how could I ever thank my Beefy, who knows every bit of my story because she helped me write it? Overwhelmed in the best way possible, I bow to my Beefy who has celebrated my life's victories and cried over my truest hurts as if they were her very own. Not sisters, something better, no doubt created for one another, I have very little doubt that this is exactly what God intended when He created Friend. As two only children, we have navigated life side by side and it is this relationship that gets the best version of myself. Nothing else mixed in, love in its purest form. Happily codependent, I could have never, ever written this without you.

My Bible study, my college sisters, Japan girls, the Sandlot Club, Inwood, MPower Boot Camp, and about two more handfuls of girls who tell the truth and make me do the same, you know you are, and I cherish you. With you I have understood and been understood, have found important things that were lost, and remembered beautiful gifts already there. Emily Dickinson said that her friends were her estate and truly, the measure of my life well spent is you.

Thank you to Rocky and Lindsey Bilhartz, who are intent on finding new ways to invest in people. To be on the receiving end of their gifts is proof of a God crazy about me. Broken sprinklers, endless pictures, babysitting and bailouts galore, Spoons nights and Lupe's porch, vacations, pizza nights, patience, service, steady consistency, ushering our baby into this world, I thank you from the bottom of my heart for what our families share. When I left Rochester to move to College Station, I was prayed over. The girls in that room put their hands on me and prayed for my first friend in my new town. It was you. He is so faithful.

Tara Seul and Samantha Scott Brantley, I am indebted ten thousand talents, an amount I could never repay. Thank you for your good eyes and honesty. I think of the combination of heart and skill necessary for such an easy hand-off and realize how blessed I am. Thank you for being the kind of people that I trust without second thought to critique what is dear to me and to love me well while doing it.

Scott Maxwell and Patty Bilhartz, I don't know how you know the things you know. I must've been absent so many days of school! Thank you for lending me your patience and precision and giving me the freedom to be my unedited self. You are wildly talented at that delicate balance and I am so grateful.

Sweet babies, Mommy's finally done! Now let's go look for bugs! Let's go jump on the trampoline! You can sing "Let it Go" as loud as your little lungs will let you! I love you, precious angels. My heart is and will always be yours. I delight in you. I am captivated by you. You amaze me with your goodness. I am so proud to be the one whom God trusted to nurture your precious spirits. Always and forever and no matter what, I love you.

And lastly, boyfriend, every good and precious gift is a gift from above, and you are simply my favorite one. This reality is better than anything I could have ever dreamed. The very best way that God loves me is using you. My truest mirror, my fire, my peace, you spur me on to do what I never thought possible, to be someone I never thought conceivable. I love you.

About Green Publishing House, LLC

Green Publishing House is a Limited Liability Company dedicated to the production and global distribution of scholarly, peer-reviewed, academic books and high quality general interest trade books. Green Publishing House partners with numerous distributors to deliver valued books across multiple platforms (digital and print) at competitive costs.

The central mission of Green Publishing House is to deliver high quality digital textbooks and trade books to readers at low prices. Going digital is not only environmentally responsible and less expensive to readers, but it also offers our clients the opportunity to receive up-to-date scholarly resources on a moment's notice from millions of locations worldwide.

Although the number of digital readers is growing every year, because everyone may not have access to the internet and eBook readers, and because some individuals, book reviewers, and libraries may prefer hard copy texts, the company also offers print copies of its books. To remain loyal to its central mission, however, the company encourages the purchase of digital versions of its books, and cheerfully donates a portion of the revenue it receives from its print copy sales to educational and charitable institutions.

31765850R00132

Made in the USA
San Bernardino, CA
18 March 2016